GCSE OCR Gateway
Physics
Higher Revision Guide

This book is for anyone doing **GCSE OCR Gateway Physics** at higher level.

GCSE Science is all about **understanding how science works**.
And not only that — understanding it well enough to be able to **question** what you hear on TV and read in the papers.

But you can't do that without a fair chunk of **background knowledge**. Hmm, tricky.

Happily this CGP book includes all the **science facts** you need to learn, and shows you how they work in the **real world**. And in true CGP style, we've explained it all as **clearly and concisely** as possible.

It's also got some daft bits in to try and make the whole experience at least vaguely entertaining for you.

What CGP is all about

Our sole aim here at CGP is to produce the highest quality books — carefully written, immaculately presented and dangerously close to being funny.

Then we work our socks off to get them out to you — at the cheapest possible prices.

Contents

MODULE P4 — RADIATION FOR LIFE

MODULE P5 — SPACE FOR REFLECTION

MODULE P6 — ELECTRICITY FOR GADGETS

EXAM SKILLS

Published by Coordination Group Publications Ltd.

From original material by Richard Parsons.

Editors:
Ellen Bowness, Gemma Hallam, Sarah Hilton, Sharon Keeley, Sam Norman, Ali Palin, Andy Park, Alan Rix, Edward Robinson, Rachel Selway, Ami Snelling, Claire Thompson, Julie Wakeling.

Contributors:
Sandy Gardner, Jason Howell, Barbara Mascetti, John Myers, Luke Waller.

ISBN: 978 1 84146 470 1

With thanks to Ian Francis and Glenn Rogers for the proofreading.
With thanks to Laura Phillips for the copyright research.

With thanks to Melissa Hull for permission to reproduce the photograph on page 4.

With thanks to Science Photo Library for permission to reproduce the photographs used on pages 5 and 26.

Data used to construct stopping distance diagram on page 40 from the Highway Code. Reproduced under the terms of the Click-Use Licence.

Graph on page 42 — based on data from *"Road Casualties Great Britain 2004: Annual Report"*, Department of Transport.

Groovy website: www.cgpbooks.co.uk

Printed by Elanders Hindson Ltd, Newcastle upon Tyne.
Jolly bits of clipart from CorelDRAW®

Moving and Storing Heat

When it starts to get a bit nippy, on goes the heating to warm things up a bit. Heating is all about the transfer of energy. Here are a few useful definitions to begin with.

Heat is a Measure of Energy

1) When a substance is heated, its particles gain energy. This energy makes the particles in a gas or a liquid move around faster. In a solid, the particles vibrate more rapidly.

2) This energy is measured on an absolute scale. (This means it can't go lower than zero, because there's a limit to how slow particles can move.) The unit of heat energy is the joule (J).

Temperature is a Measure of Hotness

1) The hotter something is, the higher its temperature.

2) Temperature is usually measured in °C (degrees Celsius), but there are other temperature scales, like °F (degrees Fahrenheit).

Energy tends to flow from hot objects to cooler ones. E.g. warm radiators heat the cold air in your room — they'd be no use if heat didn't flow.

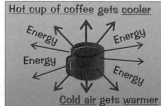

Hot cup of coffee gets cooler
Energy
Cold air gets warmer

> If there's a DIFFERENCE IN TEMPERATURE between two places, then ENERGY WILL FLOW between them.

Specific Heat Capacity Tells You How Much Energy Stuff Can Store

1) It takes more heat energy to increase the temperature of some materials than others. E.g. you need 4200 J to warm 1 kg of water by 1 °C, but only 139 J to warm 1 kg of mercury by 1 °C.

2) Materials which need to gain lots of energy to warm up also release loads of energy when they cool down again. They can 'store' a lot of heat.

3) The measure of how much energy a substance can store is called its specific heat capacity.

4) Specific heat capacity is the amount of energy needed to raise the temperature of 1 kg of a substance by 1 °C. Water has a specific heat capacity of 4200 J/kg/°C.

5) The specific heat capacity of water is high. Once water's heated, it stores a lot of energy, which makes it good for central heating systems. Also, water's a liquid so it can easily be pumped around a building.

6) You'll have to do calculations involving specific heat capacity. This is the equation to learn:

> Energy = Mass × Specific Heat Capacity × Temperature Change

EXAMPLE: How much energy is needed to heat 2 kg of water from 10 °C to 100 °C?

ANSWER: Energy needed = 2 × 4200 × 90 = 756 000 J

If you're not working out the energy, you'll have to rearrange the equation, so this formula triangle will come in dead handy.

You cover up the thing you're trying to find. The parts of the formula you can still see are what it's equal to.

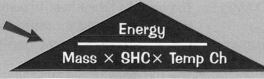

$$\frac{\text{Energy}}{\text{Mass} \times \text{SHC} \times \text{Temp Ch}}$$

EXAMPLE: An empty 200 g aluminium kettle cools down from 115 °C to 10 °C, losing 19 068 J of heat energy. What is the specific heat capacity of aluminium?

Remember — you need to convert the mass to kilograms first.

ANSWER: $\text{SHC} = \dfrac{\text{Energy}}{\text{Mass} \times \text{Temp Ch}} = \dfrac{19\,068}{0.2 \times 105} = 908\ \text{J/kg/°C}$

I wish I had a high specific fact capacity...

So there are two reasons why water's used in central heating systems — it's a liquid and it has a high specific heat capacity. This makes water good for cooling systems too. Water can absorb a lot of energy and carry it away. Water-based cooling systems are used in car engines and some computers.

Melting and Boiling

If you heat up a pan of water on the stove, the water never gets any hotter than 100 °C. You can <u>carry on heating it up</u>, but the <u>temperature won't rise</u>. How come, you say? It's all to do with <u>latent heat</u>...

You Need to Put In Energy to Break Intermolecular Bonds

1) When you heat a liquid, the <u>heat energy</u> makes the <u>particles move faster</u>. Eventually, when enough of the particles have enough energy to overcome their attraction to each other, big bubbles of <u>gas</u> form in the liquid — this is <u>boiling</u>.

2) It's similar when you heat a solid. <u>Heat energy</u> makes the <u>particles vibrate faster</u> until eventually the forces between them are overcome and the particles start to move around — this is <u>melting</u>.

3) When a substance is <u>melting</u> or <u>boiling</u>, you're still putting in <u>energy</u>, but the energy's used for <u>breaking intermolecular bonds</u> rather than raising the temperature — there are <u>flat spots</u> on the heating graph.

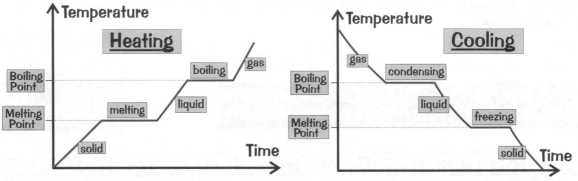

4) When a substance is <u>condensing</u> or <u>freezing</u>, bonds are <u>forming</u> between particles, which <u>releases</u> energy. This means the <u>temperature doesn't go down</u> until all the substance has turned into a liquid (condensing) or a solid (freezing).

Specific Latent Heat is the Energy Needed to Change State

1) The <u>specific latent heat of melting</u> is the <u>amount of energy</u> needed to <u>melt 1 kg</u> of material <u>without changing its temperature</u> (i.e. the material's got to be at its melting temperature already).

2) The <u>specific latent heat of boiling</u> is the <u>energy</u> needed to <u>boil 1 kg</u> of material <u>without changing its temperature</u> (i.e. the material's got to be at its boiling temperature already).

3) Specific latent heat is <u>different</u> for <u>different materials</u>, and it's different for <u>boiling</u> and <u>melting</u>. You don't have to remember what all the numbers are, though. Phew.

4) There's a <u>formula</u> to help you with all the <u>calculations</u>. And here it is:

Energy = Mass × Specific Latent Heat

* <u>EXAMPLE</u>: The specific latent heat of water (for melting) is 334 000 J/kg. How much energy is needed to melt an ice cube of mass 7 g at 0 °C?

<u>ANSWER</u>: Energy = 0.007 × 334 000 J = <u>2338 J</u>

If you're finding the mass or the specific latent heat you'll need to divide, not multiply — just to make your life a bit easier here's the formula triangle.

$$\frac{Energy}{Mass \times SLH}$$

<u>EXAMPLE</u>: The specific latent heat of water (for boiling) is 2 260 000 J/kg. 2 825 000 J of energy is used to boil dry a pan of water at 100 °C. What was the mass of water in the pan?

<u>ANSWER</u>: Mass = Energy ÷ SLH = 2 825 000 ÷ 2 260 000 J = <u>1.25 kg</u>

Breaking Bonds — Blofeld never quite manages it...

Melting a solid or boiling a liquid means you've got to <u>break bonds</u> between particles. That takes energy. Specific latent heat is just the amount of energy you need per kilogram of stuff. Incidentally, this is how <u>sweating</u> cools you down — your body heat's used to change liquid sweat into gas. Nice.

Conduction and Convection in the Home

If you build a house, there are regulations about doing it properly, mainly so that it doesn't fall down, but also so that it <u>keeps the heat in</u>. Easier said than done — there are several ways that heat is 'lost'.

Conduction Occurs Mainly in Solids

Houses lose a lot of heat through their windows even when they're shut. Heat flows from the warm inside face of the window to the cold outside face mostly by <u>conduction</u>.

1) In a <u>solid</u>, the particles are held tightly together. So when one particle <u>vibrates</u>, it <u>bumps into</u> other particles nearby and quickly passes the vibrations on.

2) Particles which vibrate <u>faster</u> than others pass on their <u>extra kinetic energy</u> (that's <u>movement</u> energy) to <u>neighbouring particles</u>. These particles then vibrate faster themselves.

3) This process continues throughout the solid and gradually the extra kinetic energy (or <u>heat</u>) is spread all the way through the solid. This causes a <u>rise in temperature</u> at the <u>other side</u>.

> **<u>CONDUCTION OF HEAT</u>** is the process where <u>vibrating particles</u> pass on <u>extra kinetic energy</u> to <u>neighbouring particles</u>.

4) <u>Metals</u> are really <u>good conductors of heat</u> — that's why they're used for <u>saucepans</u>. <u>Non-metals</u> are good for <u>insulating</u> things — e.g. for saucepan <u>handles</u>.

5) <u>Liquids and gases</u> conduct heat <u>more slowly</u> than solids — the particles aren't held so tightly together. So <u>air</u> is a good insulator.

Convection Occurs in Liquids and Gases

1) When you heat up a liquid or gas, the particles move faster, and the fluid (liquid or gas) <u>expands</u>, becoming <u>less dense</u>.

2) The <u>warmer</u>, <u>less dense</u> fluid <u>rises</u> above its <u>colder</u>, <u>denser</u> surroundings, like a hot air balloon does.

3) As the <u>warm</u> fluid <u>rises</u>, cooler fluid takes its place. As this process continues, you actually end up with a <u>circulation</u> of fluid (<u>convection currents</u>). This is how <u>immersion heaters</u> work.

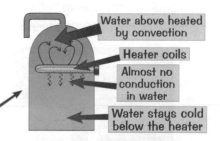

Water above heated by convection

Heater coils

Almost no conduction in water

Water stays cold below the heater

> **<u>CONVECTION</u>** occurs when the more energetic particles <u>move</u> from the <u>hotter region</u> to the <u>cooler region</u> — <u>and take their heat energy with them</u>.

4) <u>Radiators</u> in the home rely on convection to make the warm air <u>circulate</u> round the room.

5) Convection <u>can't happen in solids</u> because the <u>particles</u> <u>can't move</u> — they just vibrate on the spot.

6) To <u>reduce convection</u>, you need to <u>stop the fluid moving</u>. Clothes, blankets and cavity wall foam insulation all work by <u>trapping pockets of air</u>. The air can't move so the heat has to conduct <u>very slowly</u> through the pockets of air, as well as the material in between.

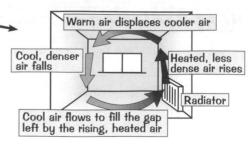

Warm air displaces cooler air

Cool, denser air falls

Heated, less dense air rises

Radiator

Cool air flows to fill the gap left by the rising, heated air

And the good old garden spade is a great example...

If a <u>garden spade</u> is left outside in cold weather, the metal bit will always feel <u>colder</u> than the wooden handle. But it <u>isn't</u> colder — it just <u>conducts heat away</u> from your hand quicker. The opposite is true if the spade is left out in the sunshine — it'll <u>feel</u> hotter because it conducts heat into your hand quicker.

Heat Radiation

Houses in Mediterranean countries are often painted white, to <u>reflect heat</u> from the Sun. In cold, cloudy Britain, we tend to leave our houses slate grey or brick red to <u>absorb</u> the heat. (Saves on paint, too.)

Radiation is How We Get Heat from the Sun

As well as by conduction and convection, heat can be transferred by <u>radiation</u>.
Heat is radiated as <u>infrared waves</u> (see p7) — they travel in <u>straight lines</u> at the <u>speed of light</u>.
<u>Radiation</u> is <u>different</u> from conduction and convection in several ways:

1) It can occur in a <u>vacuum</u>, like space. This is the <u>only way</u> that heat reaches us from the <u>Sun</u>.
2) It can only occur through <u>transparent substances</u>, like <u>air</u>, <u>glass</u> and <u>water</u>.
3) The <u>amount</u> of radiation emitted or absorbed by an object depends to a large extent on its <u>surface colour and texture</u>. This definitely <u>isn't true</u> for conduction and convection.

All Objects Emit and Absorb Heat Radiation

1) <u>All objects</u> are <u>continually</u> emitting and absorbing <u>heat radiation</u>.
2) The <u>hotter</u> an object gets, the <u>more</u> heat radiation it <u>emits</u>.
3) <u>Cooler objects</u> will <u>absorb</u> the heat radiation emitted by hotter objects around them. You can <u>feel</u> heat radiation, for example if you're indoors and the Sun shines on you through a window.
4) <u>Matt black</u> surfaces are very <u>good absorbers and emitters</u> of radiation. You should really paint your radiators black to help <u>emit</u> heat radiation, but leave your fridge a nice shiny white to help <u>reflect</u> it.
5) <u>Light-coloured, smooth</u> objects are very <u>poor absorbers and emitters</u> of radiation. They effectively <u>reflect</u> heat radiation — e.g. some people put shiny foil behind their radiators to reflect radiation back into the room rather than heat up the walls. Another good example is <u>survival blankets</u> for people rescued from snowy mountains — their shiny, smooth surface <u>reflects</u> the body heat back inside the blanket, and also <u>minimises</u> heat radiation being <u>emitted</u> by the blanket.

The shiny surface on a patio heater reflects heat downwards — onto the patio.

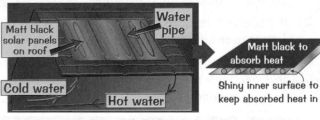

The panels for solar water heating are painted <u>matt black</u> to <u>absorb</u> as much heat as possible.

Heat Radiation is Important in Cooking

1) <u>Grills</u> and <u>toasters</u> heat food by <u>radiation</u>.
2) The heat <u>radiated</u> by a grill is absorbed by the <u>surface</u> particles of the food, increasing their <u>kinetic energy</u>. The heat energy is then <u>conducted</u> or <u>convected</u> to more central parts.
3) People often line their <u>grill pan</u> with <u>shiny foil</u>. This <u>reflects</u> the heat radiation back onto the <u>bottom</u> of the food being grilled, so the food is cooked more <u>evenly</u>. (It also stops the grill pan getting dirty, of course.)
4) <u>Over-exposure</u> to heat radiation <u>damages body cells</u> and causes <u>burning</u>.

Radiate happiness — stand by the fire and smile...

The most confusing thing about radiation is that those white things on your walls called 'radiators' actually transfer <u>most</u> of their heat by <u>convection</u>, as rising warm air. They do radiate some heat too, of course, but whoever chose the name 'radiator' obviously hadn't swotted up their physics first.

Saving Energy

It'd be daft to keep buying hamsters and letting them all escape. It's also daft to keep paying for energy to heat your house only to let the heat escape straight out again.

Insulating Your House Saves Energy and Money

1) To save energy, you need to insulate your house. It costs money to buy and install the insulation, but it also saves you money, because your heating bills are lower.

2) Eventually, the money you've saved on heating bills will equal the initial cost of installing the insulation — the time this takes is called the payback time.

3) Cheaper methods of insulation are usually less effective — they tend to save you less money per year, but they often have shorter payback times.

4) If you subtract the annual saving from the initial cost repeatedly then eventually the one with the biggest annual saving must always come out as the winner, if you think about it.

5) But you might sell the house (or die) before that happens. If you look at it over, say, a five-year period then a cheap and cheerful hot water tank jacket wins over expensive double glazing.

Loft Insulation
Fibreglass 'wool' laid across the loft floor reduces conduction through the ceiling into the roof space.
Initial Cost: £200
Annual Saving: £100
Payback time: 2 years

Hot Water Tank Jacket
Lagging such as fibreglass wool reduces conduction.
Initial Cost: £60
Annual Saving: £15
Payback time: 4 years

Cavity Walls & Insulation
Two layers of bricks with a gap between them reduce conduction. Insulating foam is squirted into the gap between layers, trapping pockets of air to minimise convection.
Initial Cost: £150
Annual Saving: £100
Payback time: 18 months

The exact costs and savings will depend on the house — but these figures give you a rough idea.

Double Glazing
Two layers of glass with an air gap between reduce conduction.
Initial Cost: £2400
Annual Saving: £80
Payback time: 30 years

Draught-proofing
Strips of foam and plastic around doors and windows stop hot air going out — reducing convection.
Initial Cost: £100
Annual Saving: £15
Payback time: 7 years

Thick Curtains
Reduce conduction and radiation through the windows.
Initial Cost: £180
Annual Saving: £20
Payback time: 9 years

Thermograms Show Where Your House is Leaking Heat

A thermogram is a picture taken with a thermal imaging camera. Objects at different temperatures emit infrared rays of different wavelengths, which the thermogram displays as different colours.

In this thermogram, red and yellow show where heat is being lost. The houses on the left and right are losing bucket-loads of heat out of their roofs, but the one in the middle must have loft insulation as it's not losing half as much.

TONY MCCONNELL/
SCIENCE PHOTO LIBRARY

It looks like this house doesn't have any double glazing either... tut, tut.

I went to a Physicist's stag night — the best man had booked a thermogram...

Insulating your house well is a really good way to save energy. Loft insulation works on exactly the same principle as you wearing that nice bobble hat that Auntie Jean knitted. Drawing the curtains is like putting on another jumper. Except people can still stare nosily at you when you've put your jumper on.

Efficiency

An open fire looks cosy, but a lot of its heat energy goes straight up the chimney, by convection, instead of heating up your living room. All this energy is 'wasted', so open fires aren't very efficient.

Machines Always Waste Some Energy

1) <u>Useful machines</u> are only <u>useful</u> because they <u>convert energy</u> from <u>one form</u> to <u>another</u>. Take cars for instance — you put in <u>chemical energy</u> (petrol or diesel) and the engine converts it into <u>kinetic (movement) energy</u>.

2) The <u>total energy output</u> is always the <u>same</u> as the <u>energy input</u>, but only some of the output energy is <u>useful</u>. So for every joule of chemical energy you put into your car you'll only get <u>a fraction of it</u> converted into useful kinetic energy.

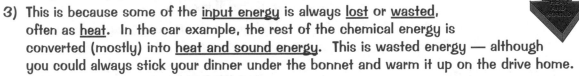

3) This is because some of the <u>input energy</u> is always <u>lost</u> or <u>wasted</u>, often as <u>heat</u>. In the car example, the rest of the chemical energy is converted (mostly) into <u>heat and sound energy</u>. This is wasted energy — although you could always stick your dinner under the bonnet and warm it up on the drive home.

4) The <u>less energy</u> that is <u>wasted</u>, the <u>more efficient</u> the device is said to be.

More Efficient Machines Waste Less Energy

The <u>efficiency</u> of a machine is defined as:

$$\text{Efficiency} = \frac{\text{USEFUL Energy OUTPUT}}{\text{TOTAL Energy INPUT}}$$

1) To work out the efficiency of a machine, first find out the <u>Total Energy INPUT</u>.

2) Then find how much <u>useful energy</u> the machine <u>delivers</u> — the <u>Useful Energy OUTPUT</u>. The question might tell you this directly, or it might tell you how much energy is <u>wasted</u> as heat/sound.

3) Then just <u>divide</u> the <u>smaller number</u> by the <u>bigger one</u> to get a value for <u>efficiency</u> somewhere between <u>0 and 1</u>. Easy. If your number is bigger than 1, you've done the division upside down.

Electric kettle

180 000 J of electrical energy supplied

9000 J of heat given out <u>to</u> the room

Think about it!

$$\text{Efficiency} = \frac{\text{Useful En. Out}}{\text{Total En. In}} = \frac{171\ 000}{180\ 000} = 0.95$$

4) You can convert the efficiency to a <u>percentage</u>, by multiplying it by 100. E.g. 0.6 = 60%.

5) In the exam you might be told the <u>efficiency</u> and asked to work out the <u>total energy input</u>, the <u>useful energy output</u> or the <u>energy wasted</u>. So you need to be able to <u>rearrange</u> the formula.

<u>EXAMPLE:</u> An ordinary light bulb is 5% efficient. If 1000 J of energy is used to light the bulb, how much energy is wasted?

<u>ANSWER:</u> Total Input $= \dfrac{\text{Useful Output}}{\text{Efficiency}} = \dfrac{1000\ \text{J}}{0.05} = 20\ 000\ \text{J}$,

so Energy Wasted = 20 000 − 1000 = <u>19 000 J</u>

Shockingly inefficient, those ordinary light bulbs. Low-energy light bulbs are roughly 4 times more efficient, and last about 8 times as long. They're more expensive though.

Efficiency = pages learned ÷ cups of tea made...

Some new appliances (like washing machines and fridges) come with a sticker with a letter from A to H on, to show how <u>energy-efficient</u> they are. A really <u>well-insulated fridge</u> might have an 'A' rating. But if you put it right next to the oven, or never defrost it, it will run much less efficiently than it should.

Electromagnetic Waves

Think about a <u>toaster</u> that <u>glows</u> when it <u>heats up</u>. It emits <u>infrared radiation</u> (heat) and a reddish <u>light</u>. You could conclude that <u>heat</u> and <u>light</u> must be similar forms of radiation. And by jingo, you'd be right. To kick things off, here's some general stuff on waves.

Waves Have Amplitude, Wavelength and Frequency

Waves have certain features:

1) The <u>amplitude</u> is the displacement from the <u>rest position</u> to the <u>crest</u>. (NOT from a trough to a crest — don't fall into that trap.)
2) The <u>wavelength</u> is the length of a <u>full cycle</u> of the wave, e.g. from <u>crest to crest</u>.
3) <u>Frequency</u> is the <u>number of complete waves</u> passing a certain point <u>per second</u>. Frequency is measured in hertz (Hz). 1 Hz is <u>1 wave per second</u>.

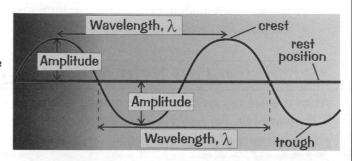

There are Seven Types of Electromagnetic (EM) Waves

Electromagnetic radiation can occur at many <u>different wavelengths</u>. In fact, there is a <u>continuous spectrum</u> of different wavelengths, but waves with <u>similar wavelengths</u> tend to have <u>similar properties</u>. Electromagnetic radiation is conventionally split into <u>seven</u> types of waves:

RADIO WAVES	MICRO WAVES	INFRA RED	VISIBLE LIGHT	ULTRA VIOLET	X-RAYS	GAMMA RAYS
$1m-10^4 m$	$10^{-2} m$ (3cm)	$10^{-5} m$ (0.01mm)	$10^{-7} m$	$10^{-8} m$	$10^{-10} m$	$10^{-12} m$

Wavelength →

1) All forms of electromagnetic radiation travel at the <u>same speed through a vacuum</u>. This means that waves with a <u>shorter wavelength</u> have a <u>higher frequency</u>.
2) As a rule the EM waves at <u>each end</u> of the spectrum tend to be able to <u>pass through material</u>, while those <u>nearer the middle</u> are <u>absorbed</u>.
3) Also, the ones with <u>higher frequency</u> (shorter wavelength), like X-rays, tend to be <u>more dangerous</u> to living cells. That's because they have more energy.
4) About half the EM radiation we receive from the <u>Sun</u> is <u>visible light</u>. Most of the rest is <u>infrared</u> (heat), with some <u>UV</u> thrown in. UV is what gives us a suntan (see page 12).

All Waves Can be Reflected, Refracted and Diffracted

When waves meet an obstacle, or pass into a different material, there are three things that might happen.

1) The waves might be <u>reflected</u> — you can only see your lovely self in the mirror because it <u>reflects</u> light.
2) They could be <u>refracted</u> — which means they <u>change direction</u> (this is why things appear to change shape when they're in water). See pages 8 & 74.
3) Or they could be <u>diffracted</u> — this means the waves 'bend round' obstacles, causing the waves to spread out. This allows waves to 'travel round corners'. See pages 9 & 71 for more on this.

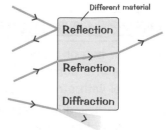

So, back to the toaster...

The toaster emits electromagnetic waves at a <u>range of different frequencies</u>, and red light and infrared radiation are both within this range of frequencies. Another example is a <u>UV insect killer</u>. It emits <u>UV radiation</u> (this is what attracts the insects), but also <u>visible light</u> and some <u>infrared</u> radiation.

Wireless Communication

In theory, any type of electromagnetic waves can be used to <u>transmit information</u>, but there are certain features of waves with <u>long wavelengths</u> that make them good for sending information long distances.

Long Wavelengths Travel Well Through Earth's Atmosphere

1) <u>Radio waves</u> and <u>microwaves</u> are good at transferring information <u>long distances</u>.

2) This is because they don't get <u>absorbed</u> by the Earth's atmosphere as much as waves in the <u>middle</u> of the EM spectrum (like heat, for example), or those at the high-frequency end of the spectrum (e.g. gamma rays or X-rays).

You couldn't use <u>high-frequency</u> waves anyway — they'd be far too <u>dangerous</u>.

Refraction Can Help Radio Waves Travel Further

When a wave comes up against something that has a <u>different density</u>, it <u>changes speed</u>. If the wave hits the new substance at an angle, it <u>changes direction</u>. This is <u>refraction</u>.

If the wave hits the boundary 'face on', it slows down but carries on in the <u>same direction</u>. It now has a shorter wavelength but the same frequency.

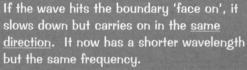

Less Dense | Denser

But if a wave meets a different medium <u>at an angle</u>, part of the wave hits the denser layer first and slows down...

Less Dense | Denser

... while another part carries on at the first, faster speed for a while. So the wave <u>changes direction</u> — it's been REFRACTED.

Now back to those radio waves:

1) UV radiation from the Sun creates layers of <u>ionised</u> atoms (atoms that have either gained or lost electrons). These <u>electrically charged</u> layers are called the <u>ionosphere</u>.

2) Radio waves travel <u>faster</u> through ionised parts of the atmosphere than non-ionised parts. This causes <u>refraction</u>.

3) <u>Medium wave</u> radio uses wavelengths of about 300 m. These radio waves are refracted most in the ionosphere — they are effectively <u>bounced back</u> to Earth. This means that <u>medium wave</u> radio signals can be received a <u>long way from the transmitter</u>.

4) The amount a wave is refracted in the ionosphere depends on its <u>frequency</u> and <u>angle of elevation</u>.

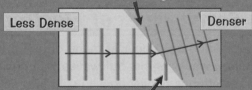

Top of wave speeds up most — Ionosphere — Bottom of wave doesn't speed up as much

Waves with a <u>higher</u> frequency or transmitted at a <u>higher angle of elevation</u> are gradually refracted back to Earth

Waves with a <u>lower</u> frequency or transmitted at a lower <u>angle of elevation</u> are refracted very quickly back to Earth

Refraction's not always good though. It can <u>disrupt</u> a signal by bending it <u>away</u> from the <u>receiver dish</u>.

Waves Can Interfere with Each Other

1) When two or more waves of a <u>similar frequency</u> come into contact, they can create one combined signal with a new <u>amplitude</u>.

2) This is called <u>interference</u>. You get it when two radio stations transmit on similar frequencies.

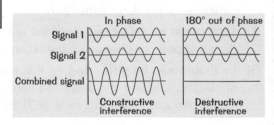

In phase | 180° out of phase
Signal 1
Signal 2
Combined signal
Constructive interference | Destructive interference

Where would Terry Wogan be without EM waves — I ask you...

In 1588, <u>beacons</u> were used on the south coast of England to <u>relay</u> the information that the Spanish Armada was approaching. As we know, <u>light</u> travels as <u>electromagnetic waves</u>, so this is an early example of transferring information using electromagnetic radiation — or <u>wireless communication</u>.

Wireless Communication & Ovens

Shorter radio waves (like the ones used for FM) don't get bounced back off the ionosphere much.
This means that the waves can't travel as far, so there need to be more transmitters.
But long wave radio can travel long distances because the waves <u>diffract</u> round the Earth.

Diffraction is When Waves Spread Out and Bend Round Corners

Here's how diffraction works.

1) All waves <u>spread out</u> at the edges when they pass through a <u>gap</u> or <u>past an object</u>. This is <u>diffraction</u>.

2) The amount of diffraction depends on the size of the gap relative to the wavelength of the wave.
The <u>narrower the gap</u>, or the <u>longer the wavelength</u>, the <u>more</u> the wave spreads out.

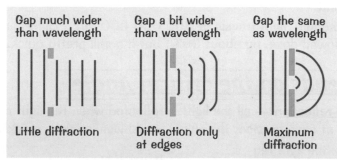

Gap much wider than wavelength — Little diffraction

Gap a bit wider than wavelength — Diffraction only at edges

Gap the same as wavelength — Maximum diffraction

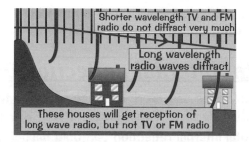

Shorter wavelength TV and FM radio do not diffract very much

Long wavelength radio waves diffract

These houses will get reception of long wave radio, but not TV or FM radio

3) Diffraction causes problems though. It can occur at the <u>edges</u> of the <u>dishes</u> used to transmit signals.
This results in <u>signal loss</u> — the wave is more spread out so the signal is <u>weaker</u>.

Microwaves Don't Diffract Much

1) Mobile phone calls travel as <u>microwaves</u> from your phone to the nearest <u>transmitter</u>.

2) Microwaves don't diffract much, so the transmitters need to be positioned in <u>line of sight</u> — they're
usually on <u>hill tops</u> and fairly <u>close to one another</u>. If there's a hill or a man-made obstacle between
your phone and the transmitter, you'll probably get a <u>poor signal</u>, or no signal at all.

3) Microwaves are also used to carry <u>satellite TV broadcasts</u> or <u>satellite phone calls</u>...

> 1) A <u>transmitter</u> on Earth sends the signal up into space...
>
> 2) ...where it's picked up by the <u>satellite receiver dish</u> orbiting thousands of
> kilometres above the Earth. The satellite transmits the signal <u>back to Earth</u>...
>
> 3) ...where it's picked up by a receiving <u>satellite dish</u>.

Microwave Ovens Use a Different Wavelength from Mobiles

1) Microwaves used for communications need to <u>pass through</u> the Earth's watery atmosphere,
but the microwaves used in <u>microwave ovens</u> have a <u>different wavelength</u>. These microwaves are
actually <u>absorbed</u> by the water molecules in the food.

2) They penetrate a few centimetres into the food before being <u>absorbed</u> by <u>water molecules</u> and
increasing their kinetic energy. The energy is then <u>conducted</u> or <u>convected</u> to other parts.

3) If microwaves are absorbed by water molecules in living tissue, <u>cells</u> may be <u>burned</u> or killed.

4) Some people think that the microwaves emitted into your body from using a mobile phone or living
near a mobile phone <u>mast</u> could also damage your <u>health</u>. There isn't any conclusive proof either
way yet though.

Concentrate — don't get diffracted...

So the key points on this page are that the <u>longer the wavelength</u>, the <u>more it diffracts</u>. This means
that long wave radio bends round the Earth, while microwaves need to be transmitted in <u>line of sight</u>.
Also you need to use microwaves of <u>different wavelengths</u> for communications and cooking.

Communicating with Light

Reflection's very useful — you can only read this book because it's reflecting light rays. But this page is really about using light to communicate over longer distances or in awkward places.

Optical Fibres Use Light or Infrared Waves

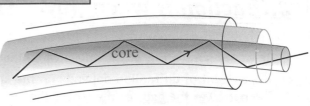

1) Optical fibres can carry data over long distances as pulses of light or infrared radiation.

2) They work by bouncing waves off the sides of a very narrow core which is protected by outer layers.

3) The light enters one end of the fibre and is reflected again and again until it emerges at the other end.

4) It's a very quick way to communicate. In a vacuum, light travels at 300 000 000 m/s. Light can't travel that fast through optical fibres — it's slowed down by about 30%, but it's still pretty quick.

Total Internal Reflection Depends on the Critical Angle

Optical fibres only work because of total internal reflection — all the light is reflected when the light ray hits the side of the inner core. If light 'escaped' at each bounce, the signal would weaken very quickly.

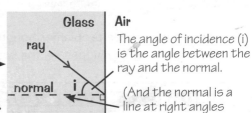

1) Total internal reflection can only happen when the light ray travels through a dense substance like glass, water or perspex towards a less dense substance like air.

2) It all depends on the angle of incidence of the ray. ⟶

3) If this angle is big enough, the ray doesn't come out at all, but reflects back into the glass (or whatever the substance is).

4) Big enough means bigger than the critical angle for that particular material — every material has its own critical angle.

The angle of incidence (i) is the angle between the ray and the normal.

(And the normal is a line at right angles to the boundary.)

If the angle of incidence is...

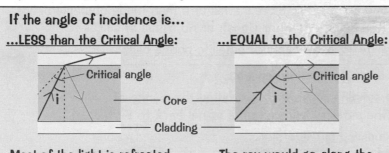

...LESS than the Critical Angle:	...EQUAL to the Critical Angle:	...GREATER than the Critical Angle:
Most of the light is refracted into the outer layer, but some of it is internally reflected.	The ray would go along the surface (with quite a bit of internal reflection as well).	No light comes out. It's all internally reflected, i.e. total internal reflection.

Different Sorts of Signals Have Different Advantages

1) Communicating with light, radio and electrical signals (like you get in an ordinary phone line) is great because the signals travel really fast.

2) Electrical wires and optical fibres can carry loads of information really quickly — see page 76.

3) Communications sent through optical fibres and electrical wires are pretty secure — they're inside a cable and so can't easily be tapped in to. Radio signals travel through the air, so they can be intercepted more easily. This is an issue for people using wireless internet networks.

4) Cables can be difficult to repair if they get broken. This isn't a problem for wireless communication.

If you're not sure what life's about, try total internal reflection...

Here's something to make you go 'wow...' in amazement — an optical fibre, which is thinner than a human hair, can have over one million telephone calls going down it at the same time.

Digital Technology

Going back to the Spanish Armada example, it didn't matter <u>how bright</u> the beacons were — as long as they could be seen. They were either 'on' or 'off'. This is the principle behind digital technology.

Analogue Signals Vary but Digital's Just On or Off

1) An <u>analogue</u> wave can take <u>any</u> value within a certain range. (Remember: <u>a</u>nalogue — <u>any</u>.)

2) A <u>digital</u> signal can only take <u>two</u> values. These values tend to be called <u>on/off</u>, or <u>1/0</u>. For example, you can send data along optical fibres as short <u>pulses</u> of light.

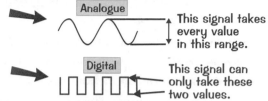

Analogue — This signal takes every value in this range.

Digital — This signal can only take these two values.

Digital Signals Have Advantages over Analogue

1) Both digital and analogue signals <u>weaken</u> as they travel, so they need to be <u>amplified</u> along their route. Interference also causes <u>random disturbances</u>, called <u>noise</u>, which can lead to a poor quality signal.

2) When you amplify an <u>analogue</u> signal, the low-amplitude <u>noise</u> is amplified too. So every time it's amplified, the signal loses quality.

3) With a <u>digital</u> signal, the low-amplitude noise is just <u>ignored</u>. So the signal remains <u>high quality</u>.

DIGITAL:

This noisy digital signal... ...is obviously supposed to be this.

ANALOGUE:

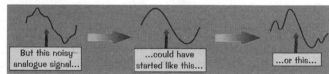

But this noisy analogue signal... ...could have started like this... ...or this...

4) Another advantage of digital technology is that you can transmit <u>several signals</u> at the <u>same time</u> using just one cable or EM wave — this is called <u>multiplexing</u>.

5) Multiplexing happens in <u>phone wires</u>. When you're on the phone, your voice is converted into a digital signal and transmitted regularly at <u>very small time intervals</u>. In between your voice signals being transmitted, thousands of other people's voice signals can be <u>slotted in</u> or '<u>multiplexed</u>'. The samples are <u>separated out</u> again at the other end so the person you called can hear you — and only you. This happens so quickly that you don't notice it.

CD Players Use Lasers to Read Digital Information

1) The surface of a CD has a pattern of shallow <u>pits</u> cut into it. The areas between the pits are called <u>lands</u>.

They seem like pits when you look from the top, anyway. But the laser shines from underneath, so it sees the pits as slightly <u>raised</u> areas.

2) A laser shone onto the CD is <u>reflected</u> from the shiny surface as it spins around in the player.

3) The beam is reflected from a <u>land</u> and a <u>pit</u> slightly <u>differently</u> — and this difference can be picked up by a <u>light sensor</u>. These differences in reflected signals can then be changed into an <u>electrical signal</u>.

Cross section of CD
Plastic disk
Land — Pit
Laser shines from underneath

4) The pits and lands themselves don't represent the digital <u>ons</u> and <u>offs</u>. It's actually a <u>change</u> in the reflected beam which represents <u>on</u>, while <u>no change</u> represents <u>off</u>.

5) An <u>amplifier</u> and a <u>loudspeaker</u> then convert the electrical signal into <u>sound</u> of the right pitch (frequency) and loudness.

C Dese pages — they're important, so learn them...

All right, so CDs haven't been cutting-edge technology since you were in nappies — but they're a good example of digital technology to write about in your exam. You also need to remember that digital signals let you send <u>more data</u> down one cable than analogue, and with <u>less 'noise'</u>.

Humans and the Environment

Sunbathing all day can be really bad for you, especially if you're pale skinned. So if you're reading this outside on a hot summer's day, find a floppy hat and slap some sunscreen on.

Ultraviolet Radiation Causes Skin Cancer

1) If you spend a lot of time in the <u>Sun</u>, you can expect to get a <u>tan</u> and maybe <u>sunburn</u>.

2) But the more time you spend in the Sun, the more chance you also have of getting <u>skin cancer</u>. This is because the Sun's rays include <u>ultraviolet radiation</u> (UV) which damages the DNA in your cells.

3) <u>Dark skin</u> gives some protection against UV rays — it <u>absorbs</u> more UV radiation. This prevents some of the damaging radiation from reaching the more <u>vulnerable</u> tissues deeper in the body.

4) Everyone should protect themselves from the Sun, but if you're pale skinned, you need to take extra care, and use a sunscreen with a higher <u>Sun Protection Factor</u> (SPF).

5) An <u>SPF</u> of <u>15</u> means you can spend <u>15 times as long</u> as you otherwise could in the Sun <u>without burning</u> (as long as you keep reapplying the sunscreen).

<u>EXAMPLE:</u>   Ruvani normally burns after 40 minutes in the Sun. Before going to the beach, she applies sunscreen with SPF 8. For how long can she sunbathe before she will start to burn?

<u>ANSWER:</u>   Time = 40 mins × 8 = 320 minutes = 5 hours and 20 minutes.

The Ozone Layer Protects Us from UV Radiation

1) <u>Ozone</u> is a molecule made of <u>three oxygen atoms</u>, O_3. There's a <u>layer</u> of ozone <u>high up</u> in the Earth's atmosphere.

2) The ozone layer <u>absorbs</u> some of the <u>UV rays</u> from the <u>Sun</u> — so it <u>reduces</u> the amount of UV radiation reaching the Earth's <u>surface</u>.

3) Recently, the ozone layer has got <u>thinner</u> because of pollution from <u>CFCs</u> — these are <u>gases</u> which <u>react</u> with <u>ozone</u> molecules and <u>break them up</u>. This <u>depletion</u> of the ozone layer allows <u>more UV rays</u> to reach us at the surface of the Earth.

4) We used to use CFCs all the time — e.g. in hairsprays and in the coolant for fridges — they're now <u>banned</u> or <u>restricted</u> because of their environmental impact.

Natural Events and Human Activities Affect Weather Patterns

The Earth's atmosphere has a huge impact on the amount of EM radiation that reaches the Earth's surface, and how much radiation is able to escape back into space. This in turn affects our <u>weather</u> and <u>climate</u>.

1) In cities, buildings <u>absorb</u> and <u>store</u> heat (see page 4) during the day and then release it at night. But <u>dust pollution</u> (from traffic, factories, etc.) acts like a <u>blanket</u> at night, <u>trapping</u> heat radiation. So cities tend to be <u>warmer</u> than the countryside around them.

2) When a <u>volcano</u> erupts, a lot of dust can shoot up <u>high</u> into the atmosphere. This dust reflects radiation from the Sun. Less radiation gets through to the Earth, which <u>cools down</u> as a result.

> Natural events and human activity can also change the <u>climate</u> on a <u>global</u> scale. For example:
> • Changes in the Earth's orbit around the Sun can help to cause <u>ice ages</u>.
> • The scientific consensus is that human activities are causing <u>climate change</u> — especially <u>emission of carbon dioxide</u> and other 'greenhouse gases', which trap heat from the Sun.

Use protection — wear a hat...

Okay... time for a bit of <u>risk balancing</u>. <u>Too much</u> time in the Sun can help cause skin cancer, but that doesn't mean you want to avoid sunshine <u>completely</u>. A bit of sun can be a <u>good thing</u> (it helps with your body's production of <u>vitamin D</u>). Being <u>sensible</u> and not going mad is probably the best policy.

Using the Wave Equation

There's a very simple equation which connects the <u>frequency</u>, <u>wavelength</u> and <u>speed</u> of a wave. It works for any wave. All you have to do is learn the equation and practise using it.

Wave Speed = Frequency × Wavelength

You need to learn this equation — it's not given in the exam.

$$\text{Speed} = \text{Frequency} \times \text{Wavelength}$$
$$\text{(m/s)} \qquad \text{(Hz)} \qquad \text{(m)}$$

OR

$$v = f\lambda$$

Speed (v is for <u>velocity</u>)

Frequency

Wavelength (that's the Greek letter 'lambda')

EXAMPLE: Eva is building a sandcastle. She estimates that 1 wave passes her sandcastle every 2 seconds, and that the crests of the waves are 90 cm apart. Calculate the speed, in metres per second, of the waves passing Eva's sandcastle.

In <u>one second</u>, <u>half a wave</u> passes, so the frequency is <u>0.5 Hz</u> (hertz).

ANSWER: Speed = 0.5 × 0.90 = <u>0.45 m/s</u>
(Remember to change the 90 cm into metres first.)

You might be asked to calculate the <u>frequency</u> or <u>wavelength</u> instead of the speed though, so you need the good old <u>triangle</u> too...

You Need to Convert Your Units First

1) The <u>standard (SI) units</u> involved in wave equations are: <u>metres</u>, <u>seconds</u>, <u>m/s</u> and <u>hertz (Hz)</u>.

Always CONVERT INTO SI UNITS (m, s, m/s, Hz) before you work anything out.

2) The trouble is waves often have <u>high frequencies</u> given in <u>kHz</u> or <u>MHz</u>, so make sure you <u>learn this</u> too:

1 kHz (kilohertz) = 1000 Hz   1 MHz (1 megahertz) = 1 000 000 Hz

3) <u>Wavelengths</u> can also be given in <u>other units</u>, e.g. <u>km</u> for long-wave radio.

4) There's worse still: The <u>speed of light</u> is 3×10^8 <u>m/s</u> = <u>300 000 000 m/s</u>. This, along with numbers like <u>900 MHz</u> = <u>900 000 000 Hz</u> won't fit into some calculators. That leaves you <u>three choices</u>:

   1) Enter the numbers as <u>standard form</u>. For example, to enter 3×10^8, press [3] [EXP] [8]. (Your calculator might have a different button for standard form — if you don't know what it is, find out...)

   2) <u>Cancel</u> three or six <u>noughts</u> off both numbers (so long as you're <u>dividing</u> them!) or...

   3) Do it entirely <u>without a calculator</u> (no really, I've seen it done).

EXAMPLE: A radio wave has a frequency of 92.2 MHz. Find its wavelength. (The speed of all EM waves is 3×10^8 m/s.)

ANSWER: You're trying to find λ using f and v, so you've got to rearrange the equation. You need to convert the frequency into the SI unit, Hz: 92.2 MHz = 92 200 000 Hz
So $\lambda = v \div f = 3 \times 10^8 \div 92\,200\,000 = 3 \times 10^8 \div 9.22 \times 10^7 = $ <u>3.25 m</u>

It's probably easiest to use standard form here.

This stuff on formulas is really painful — I mean it MHz...

Learn the main rules on this page, then <u>cover it up</u> and <u>scribble them down</u>. Then try these:
1) A sound wave has a frequency of 2500 Hz and a wavelength of 13.2 cm. Find its speed.
2) A radio wave has a wavelength of 3 m. Find its frequency.

N.B. You can find the answers to these questions on page 100.

Seismic Waves

You can't drill very far into the crust of the Earth (only about 12 km), so scientists use <u>seismic waves</u> produced by earthquakes to investigate the Earth's inner structure.

Earthquakes Cause Different Types of Seismic Waves

1) When there's an <u>earthquake</u> somewhere, it produces <u>shock waves</u> which travel out through the Earth. We <u>record</u> these <u>seismic waves</u> all over the <u>surface</u> of the planet using <u>seismographs</u>.

2) <u>Seismologists</u> measure the <u>time</u> it takes for the shock waves to reach each seismograph.

3) They also note which parts of the Earth <u>don't receive the shock waves</u> at all.

4) There are <u>two different types</u> of seismic waves that travel through the Earth — <u>P-waves</u> and <u>S-waves</u>.

P-Waves are Longitudinal

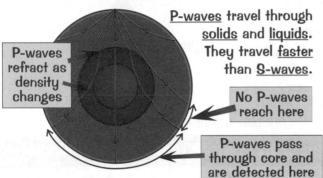

Longitudinal waves
The vibrations are along the direction that the wave travels.

Vibrations this way ←→
Wave travelling this way ➔

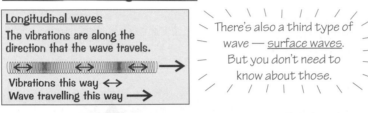

There's also a third type of wave — <u>surface waves</u>. But you don't need to know about those.

S-Waves are TranSverSe

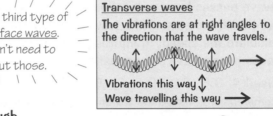

Transverse waves
The vibrations are at right angles to the direction that the wave travels.

Vibrations this way ↕
Wave travelling this way ➔

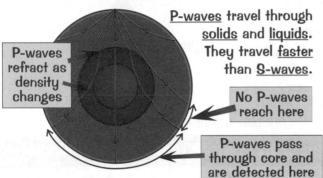

<u>P-waves</u> travel through <u>solids</u> and <u>liquids</u>. They travel <u>faster</u> than <u>S-waves</u>.

P-waves refract as density changes

No P-waves reach here

P-waves pass through core and are detected here

<u>S-waves</u> only travel through <u>Solids</u>. They are <u>Slower</u> than <u>P-waves</u>.

No S waves reach here — they can't pass through the liquid outer core

The Seismograph Results Tell Us What's Down There

1) About <u>halfway through</u> the Earth, P-waves <u>change direction</u> abruptly. This indicates that there's a <u>sudden change</u> in <u>properties</u> — as you go from the <u>mantle</u> to the <u>core</u>.

2) The fact that <u>S-waves</u> are <u>not detected</u> in the core's <u>shadow</u> tells us that the <u>outer core</u> is <u>liquid</u> — <u>S</u> waves only pass through <u>Solids</u>.

3) <u>P-waves</u> seem to travel <u>slightly faster</u> through the <u>middle</u> of the core, which strongly suggests that there's a <u>solid inner core</u>.

4) Note that <u>S-waves</u> do travel through the <u>mantle</u>, which shows that it's <u>solid</u>. It only melts to form magma in small 'hot spots'.

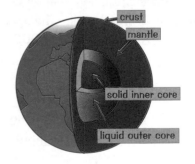

crust
mantle
solid inner core
liquid outer core

The Waves Curve with Increasing Depth

1) The <u>waves</u> change speed as the <u>properties</u> of the mantle and core change.
2) This change in speed causes the waves to change direction — which is <u>refraction</u>, of course.
3) Most of the time the waves change speed <u>gradually</u>, resulting in a <u>curved</u> path.
4) But when the properties change <u>suddenly</u>, the wave speed changes abruptly, and the path has a <u>kink</u>.

Seismic waves — they reveal the terrible trembling truth...

Seismic waves are very different from all the electromagnetic waves on the previous pages. You need to learn all the details about both types of seismic waves — whether they're <u>transverse</u> or <u>longitudinal</u>, if they pass through solids <u>and</u> liquids or <u>just</u> solids, and which is <u>faster</u>. Learn, scribble and enjoy.

Revision Summary for Module P1

And that's the first bout of Physics — but it's not quite over yet. You've got to check that what you think you learned actually stuck in your brain. The best way to do that is by answering all these lovely questions. There are four formulas to learn to use in this section. Watch out for units though — before you bung your numbers into the formulas you have to make sure they're in the right units. It's a big pitfall, so don't fall head first into it. Anyway, enough gasbagging — off you go.

1) Explain the difference between heat and temperature. What units are they each measured in?

2) * A rod of metal has a mass of 600 g. It's heated from 18 °C to 28 °C using 5400 J. Calculate the specific heat capacity of the metal.

3) Why does a graph showing the temperature of a substance as it's heated have two flat bits?

4) * The specific latent heat of water (for boiling) is 2.26×10^6 J/kg. How much energy does it take to boil dry a kettle containing 350 g of boiling water?

5) Describe the process that transfers heat energy through a metal rod. What is this process called?

6) Describe how the heat from an immersion heater is transferred throughout the water in a tank. What is this process called?

7) Explain why solar hot water panels have a matt black surface.

8) Explain how the design of a mug could be changed so that it keeps its contents warmer for longer.

9) Name five ways of reducing the amount of heat lost from a house, and explain how they work.

10)* The following table gives some information about two different energy-saving light bulbs.

a) What is the payback time for light bulb A?
b) Which light bulb is more cost-effective over one year?

	Price of bulb	Annual saving
Light bulb A	£2.50	£1.25
Light bulb B	£3.00	£2.00

11) What does a thermogram show?

12)* What is the efficiency of a motor that converts 100 J of electrical energy into 70 J of useful energy?

13) Draw a diagram of a wave and label a crest and a trough, and the wavelength and amplitude.

14) Sketch the EM spectrum with all the details you've learned. Put the lowest frequency waves on the left.

15) Which is generally more dangerous — low frequency or high frequency EM radiation?

16) Describe the different ways that short, medium and long-wave radio signals travel.

17) Draw a diagram showing the diffraction of a wave as it passes through: a) a small gap, b) a big gap.

18) Explain what refraction is and how it can disrupt radio signals.

19) Describe how microwave ovens cook food.

20) a) Which two types of EM wave are commonly used to send signals along optical fibres?
b) Explain why sending data by optical fibre might be better than broadcasting it as a radio signal.

21)* In which of the cases A to D below would the ray of light be totally internally reflected? (The critical angle for glass is approximately 42°.)

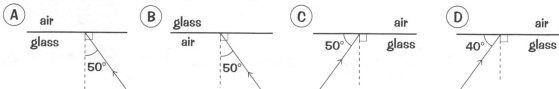

22) Draw diagrams illustrating analogue and digital signals. Give two advantages of digital signals.

23) How are lasers used in CD players?

24) What has led to a thinning of the ozone layer? Why is this a problem for humans?

25) How might a volcanic eruption change the climate of the Earth?

26)* Convert to SI units (m, m/s, Hz, s): a) 500 kHz, b) 35 cm, c) 4.6 MHz, d) 4 cm/s, e) 2½ mins.

27)* Find the speed of a wave with frequency 50 kHz and wavelength 0.3 cm.

28) How do P-waves and S-waves differ regarding: a) type of wave, b) speed, c) what they go through?

29) Why do P-waves and S-waves change direction as they travel through the Earth?

Using the Sun's Energy

The Sun is <u>very</u> hot and <u>very</u> bright — which means it's kicking out a <u>lot</u> of energy.

The Sun is the Ultimate Source of Loads of Our Energy

1) <u>Every second</u> for the last few billion years or so, the Sun has been giving out <u>loads</u> of <u>energy</u> — mostly in the form of <u>heat</u> and <u>light</u>.

2) Some of that energy is <u>stored</u> here on Earth as <u>fossil fuels</u> (coal, oil and gas). And when we use wind power, we're using energy that can be <u>traced back</u> to the Sun (the Sun heats the <u>air</u>, the <u>hot air rises</u>, cold air <u>whooshes in</u> to take its place (wind), and so on).

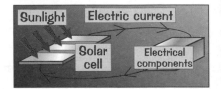

Fossil fuels are the remains of plants and animals that lived millions of years ago.

3) But we can also use the Sun's energy in a more <u>direct</u> way — with <u>solar cells</u> and <u>solar heating</u>.

You Can Capture the Sun's Energy Using Solar Cells

1) <u>Solar cells</u> (<u>photocells</u>) generate <u>electricity directly</u> from sunlight.

2) They generate <u>direct current</u> (DC) — the same as a <u>battery</u>. Direct current just means the current flows the <u>same way</u> round the circuit all the time — not like <u>mains electricity</u> in your home (AC), which keeps <u>switching</u> direction (see page 18).

Sunlight	Electric current
Solar cell	Electrical components

3) Solar cells are made of <u>silicon</u> — a <u>semiconductor</u>. When sunlight falls on the cell:
i) the silicon atoms <u>absorb</u> some of the energy, knocking loose some <u>electrons</u>,
ii) these electrons then flow round a circuit — which is electricity.

4) The <u>power output</u> of a photocell depends on its <u>surface area</u> (the bigger the cell, the more electricity it produces) and the <u>intensity of the sunlight</u> hitting it (brighter light = more power). Makes sense.

Photocells have <u>lots of advantages</u>:
• There are no moving parts — so they're <u>sturdy</u>, <u>low maintenance</u> and last a <u>long time</u>.
• You don't need <u>power cables</u> or <u>fuel</u> (your digital calculator doesn't need to be plugged in/fuelled up).
• Solar power won't run out (it's a <u>renewable</u> energy resource), and it <u>doesn't pollute</u> the environment.

But there's <u>one major disadvantage</u> — <u>no sunlight</u>, <u>no power</u>.
So they're rubbish at night, and not so good when the weather's bad.

Passive Solar Heating — No Complex Mechanical Stuff

SOLAR PANELS

Solar panels are much less sophisticated than photocells — basically just <u>black water pipes</u> inside a <u>glass</u> box. The <u>glass</u> lets <u>heat</u> and <u>light</u> from the Sun in — but, just like in a greenhouse, it can't get back out so easily.

This heat and light is then <u>absorbed</u> by the black pipes and heats up the water (which can be used for <u>washing</u> or pumped to <u>radiators</u> to heat the building).

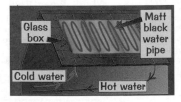

Labels: Glass box, Matt black water pipe, Cold water, Hot water

CAREFULLY DESIGNED BUILDINGS CAN USE ENERGY MORE EFFICIENTLY

You can reduce the energy needed to <u>heat</u> a building if you build it sensibly in the first place — e.g. it can make a big difference which way the <u>windows</u> face.

All the radiation that lands on the curved mirror is focused right on your pan.

COOKING WITH SOLAR POWER

If you get a <u>curved mirror</u>, then you can <u>focus</u> the Sun's light and heat. This is what happens in a solar oven.

Don't let the Sun go down on me — I hate cold showers...

The more directly a solar panel faces the Sun, the more energy it'll absorb. So to improve the efficiency of a solar panel, you can make it <u>track</u> the position of the <u>Sun</u> in the sky. Although <u>initial costs</u> can be <u>high</u> with solar power, once you're up and running, the energy is <u>free</u> and <u>running costs almost nil</u>.

Producing and Distributing Electricity

Most of our electricity is generated in <u>power stations</u> and then distributed via the <u>National Grid</u>.

The National Grid Connects Power Stations to Consumers

1) The <u>National Grid</u> is the <u>network</u> of pylons and cables which covers <u>the whole country</u>.

2) It takes electricity from <u>power stations</u> to just where it's needed in <u>homes</u> and <u>industry</u>.

3) It enables power to be <u>generated</u> anywhere on the grid, and then <u>supplied</u> anywhere else on the grid. (See also page 91.)

All Power Stations are Pretty Much the Same...

1) The aim of a <u>power station</u> is to <u>convert</u> one kind of energy (e.g. the energy stored in fossil fuels, or nuclear energy contained in the centre of atoms) into <u>electricity</u>.

2) Usually this is done in <u>three stages</u>...

① The first stage is to use the <u>fuel</u> (e.g. gas or nuclear fuel) to generate <u>steam</u> — this is the job of the <u>boiler</u>.

② The moving steam drives the blades of a <u>turbine</u>...

③ ...and this rotating movement from the turbine is converted to <u>electricity</u> by the <u>generator</u> (using <u>electromagnetic induction</u> — see the next page).

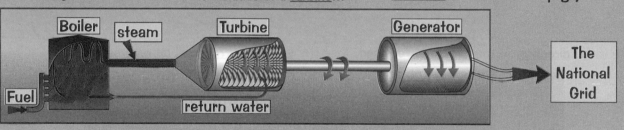

3) Most power stations are terribly <u>inefficient</u> — usually more than half the energy produced is <u>wasted</u> as <u>heat and noise</u> (though the efficiency of the power station depends a lot on the <u>power source</u>).

...It's the Method of Generating the Heat That Changes

In the UK, most power stations use <u>fossil fuels</u> (oil, coal and gas) or <u>nuclear fuel</u> to generate heat. But there are a few that use <u>biomass</u> — stuff from <u>plants</u> (like wood and straw) or <u>animals</u> (their <u>manure</u>).

FOSSIL FUELS Fossil fuels are <u>burned</u> to release their heat energy. At the moment, these fuels are readily available, and they're a <u>concentrated</u> source of energy (a little bit of coal gives a lot of heat).

But burning fossil fuels causes <u>acid rain</u> and produces <u>carbon dioxide</u> (a greenhouse gas — see page 12). Also, we buy most of our fossil fuels from other countries — which means we don't have control of the <u>price</u> or <u>supply</u>. (Plus they're <u>running out</u>, of course.)

NUCLEAR POWER <u>Nuclear</u> power stations use the heat released by <u>uranium</u> atoms as they split during a nuclear reaction. There's a lot more about nuclear power on pages 21 & 62.

BIOMASS Biomass is usually <u>fermented</u> to produce <u>methane</u>. The methane is then used to make '<u>biofuels</u>', which can be burned.

Biomass is <u>renewable</u> — we can <u>quickly</u> make more by planting more trees and rearing more animals. Burning methane does produce <u>carbon dioxide</u>, but this is CO_2 that the plants took <u>out</u> of the atmosphere when they were growing — the process is '<u>carbon neutral</u>' overall.

Recently, we've started to use biomass more in the UK. You do need a lot of biomass to replace one lump of coal, <u>but</u> we don't need to import straw and poo from other countries.

Power stations — nothing to get steamed up about...

Not all power stations use <u>steam</u> to turn the blades of a turbine. For example, windmills (a better name is <u>wind turbines</u>) turn the turbine directly. But once the turbine's turning, the rest of the details are more or less the same. Carry on reading to find out how the <u>generator</u> works...

The Dynamo Effect

Generators use a pretty cool piece of physics to make **electricity** from the **movement** of a turbine. It's called **electromagnetic (EM) induction** — which basically means making **electricity** using a **magnet**.

ELECTROMAGNETIC INDUCTION: The creation of a **VOLTAGE** (and maybe current) in a wire which is experiencing a **CHANGE IN MAGNETIC FIELD**.

The Dynamo Effect — Move the Wire or the Magnet

1) Using **electromagnetic induction** to transform **kinetic energy** (energy of moving things) into **electrical energy** is called the **dynamo effect**. (In a power station, this kinetic energy is provided by the **turbine**.)

2) There are two different situations where you get EM induction:
   a) An **electrical conductor** (a coil of wire is often used) **moves** through a **magnetic field**.
   b) The **magnetic field** through an **electrical conductor changes** (gets bigger or smaller or reverses).

Electrical conductor moving in a magnetic field.

Induced voltage

Magnetic field through a conductor changing (as the magnet moves).

3) If the **direction** of movement is **reversed**, then the **voltage/current** will be **reversed** too.

To get a **bigger voltage**, you can increase...
1) The **STRENGTH** of the **MAGNET**
2) The **number of TURNS** on the **COIL**
3) The **SPEED** of movement

Generators Move a Coil in a Magnetic Field

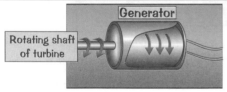

Generator

Rotating shaft of turbine

1) Generators **rotate a coil** in a **magnetic field**.

2) Every half a turn, the current in the coil **swaps direction**. (Think about one part of the coil... sometimes it's heading for the magnet's north pole, sometimes for the south — it changes every half a turn. This is what makes the current change direction.)

3) This means that generators produce an **alternating (AC) current**. If you looked at the current (or voltage) on a display, you'd see something like this...

   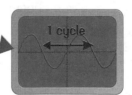

   1 cycle

   Turning the coil **faster** produces not only **more** peaks, but a **higher voltage** too.

4) The **frequency** of AC electrical supplies is the number of 'cycles' per second, and is measured in **hertz** (Hz). In the UK, electricity is supplied at 50 Hz (which means the coil in the generator at the power station is rotating 50 times every second).

5) Remember, this is completely different from the DC electricity supplied by batteries and solar cells. If you plotted that on a graph, you'd see something more like this...

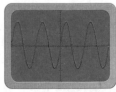

6) **Dynamos** on bikes work slightly differently — they usually rotate the **magnet** near the coil. But the principle is **exactly the same** — they're still using EM induction.

A conductor moving in a field — must be an open-air concert...

EM induction sounds pretty hard, but it boils down to this — if a **magnetic field changes** (moves, grows, shrinks... whatever) somewhere near a **conductor**, you get **electricity**. It's a weird old thing, but important — this is how all our mains electricity is generated.

Supplying Electricity Efficiently

Pumping electricity round the country is best done at <u>high voltage</u>.
This is why you probably weren't encouraged to climb electricity pylons as a child.

Electricity is Transformed to High Voltage Before Distribution

1) To transmit a lot of electrical power, you either need a <u>high voltage</u> or a <u>high current</u> (see page 91 for more info about why). But... a higher current means your cables get hot, which is very inefficient (all that heat just goes to waste).

2) It's much cheaper to <u>increase</u> the <u>voltage</u>. So before the electricity is sent round the country, the voltage is transformed to <u>400 000 V</u>. (This keeps the current very <u>low</u>, meaning less wasted energy.)

3) To increase the voltage, you need a <u>step-up transformer</u>.

4) Even though you need big <u>pylons</u> with <u>huge</u> insulators (as well as the transformers themselves), using a high voltage is the <u>cheapest</u> way to transmit electricity.

5) To bring the voltage down to <u>safe usable levels</u> for homes, there are local <u>step-down transformers</u> scattered round towns — for example, look for a little fenced-off shed with signs all over it saying "Keep Out" and "Danger of Death".

6) This is the main reason why mains electricity is AC — so that the <u>transformers</u> work. Transformers <u>only work</u> on <u>AC</u>.

Power Stations aren't Very Efficient

1) The process of generating and supplying electricity <u>isn't</u> massively efficient.

2) Unfortunately most power stations produce a lot of <u>waste energy</u> (e.g. heat lost to the <u>environment</u>) as well as energy we can make use of. Basically the energy in each bit of fuel is broken down into <u>two parts</u> — the '<u>useful bit</u>' and the '<u>wasted bit</u>'. Learn this equation...

The <u>total</u> energy output is <u>always</u> the same as the energy input.

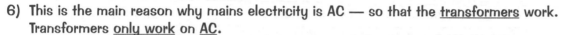

FUEL Energy Input = ELECTRICAL energy output + WASTE energy output

3) There's an equation for working out <u>efficiency</u> as well... yep, learn this one too:

$$\text{Efficiency} = \frac{\text{ELECTRICAL Energy OUTPUT}}{\text{FUEL Energy INPUT}}$$

Here's the formula triangle for the efficiency equation. As always, cover up the thing you want to find out — what you can still see is the formula that'll tell you how to get it.

EXAMPLE: A coal-fired power station generates 200 MJ (200 000 000 J) of electrical energy per second. 450 MJ of energy is wasted per second as heat and noise.

Calculate: a) the energy used by the power station in a second,
b) the efficiency of the power station.

ANSWER: a) Energy used (energy input) = energy output + energy wasted
= 200 MJ + 450 MJ = <u>650 MJ</u>

b) Efficiency = energy output ÷ energy input = 200 ÷ 650 = <u>0.3077</u> (or 30.77%).

All that energy — straight down the grid...

Once you've <u>generated</u> all that electricity, you don't want to <u>waste it</u> by heating up miles and miles of power cables when you're <u>distributing</u> it. So keep the <u>current</u> in the power cables <u>low</u>, and make the voltage <u>high</u>. Then the good folk of John o' Groats can still afford to boil the kettle. Problem solved.

Electrical Power

Electrical power is the <u>amount of energy converted per second</u>. It's a hoot.

Running Costs Depend on an Appliance's Power Rating

1) Power's measured in <u>watts</u> (W) or <u>kilowatts</u> (kW) — where <u>1 watt means 1 joule per second</u>.

   For example, a light bulb with a power rating of 100 W uses 100 J of electrical energy <u>every second</u>. And a 2 kW kettle converts electrical energy at the rate of 2000 J <u>per second</u>. Easy.

2) If they're both on for the same amount of <u>time</u>, the <u>kettle</u> is much more <u>expensive</u> to run than the bulb, because it consumes more energy (and it's <u>energy</u> you pay for — see below).

3) The <u>power rating</u> of an appliance depends on the <u>voltage</u> and the <u>current</u> it uses. Equation time...

So to transmit a lot of power, you need either high voltage or high current — see pages 19 & 91.

$$\text{Power (in W)} = \text{Voltage (in V)} \times \text{Current (in A)}$$

You know the drill — learn: (i) <u>the equation</u>, and (ii) <u>how to rearrange it</u>.

EXAMPLE: Find the current flowing through a 100 W light bulb if the voltage is 230 V.
ANSWER: Current = Power ÷ Voltage = 100 ÷ 230 = 0.43 amps

Kilowatt-hours (kWh) are "UNITS" of Energy

Your electricity meter records how much <u>energy</u> you use in units of <u>kilowatt-hours</u>, or <u>kWh</u>.

A <u>KILOWATT-HOUR</u> is the amount of electrical energy converted by a <u>1 kW appliance</u> left on for <u>1 HOUR</u>.

The <u>higher</u> the <u>power rating</u> of an appliance, and the <u>longer</u> you leave it on, the more energy it consumes, and the more it costs. Learn (and practise rearranging) this equation too...

$$\underset{\text{(in kWh)}}{\text{UNITS OF ENERGY}} = \underset{\text{(in kW)}}{\text{POWER}} \times \underset{\text{(in hours)}}{\text{TIME}}$$

And this one (but this one's easy): **COST = NUMBER OF UNITS × PRICE PER UNIT**

EXAMPLE: Find the cost of leaving a 60 W light bulb on for 30 minutes if one kWh costs 10p.
ANSWER: Energy (in kWh) = Power (in kW) × Time (in hours) = 0.06 kW × ½ hr = <u>0.03 kWh</u>
Cost = number of units × price per unit = 0.03 × 10p = <u>0.3p</u>

Off-Peak Electricity is Cheaper

Electricity supplied <u>during the night</u> (off-peak) is sometimes cheaper. <u>Storage heaters</u> take advantage of this — they heat up at night and then release the heat slowly throughout the day. If you can put <u>washing machines</u>, <u>dishwashers</u>, etc. on at night, so much the better.

<u>ADVANTAGES</u> of using off-peak electricity	<u>DISADVANTAGES</u> of using off-peak electricity
1) <u>Cost-effective</u> for the electricity company — power stations can't be turned off at night, so it's good if there's a demand for electricity at night. 2) <u>Cheaper</u> for consumers if they buy electricity during the <u>off-peak</u> hours.	1) There's a slightly increased <u>risk of fire</u> with more appliances going at night but no one watching. 2) You start fitting your <u>routine</u> around the <u>cheap rate</u> hours — i.e. you might stop enjoying the use of electricity during the day.

Watt's the answer — well, part of it...

Get a bit of <u>practice</u> with the equations in those lovely bright red boxes, and try these questions:
1) A kettle draws a current of 12 A from the 230 V mains supply. Calculate its power rating.
2) With 0.5 kWh of energy, for how long could you run the kettle?

Answers on page 100.

Power Sources for the Future

Everyone knows <u>fossil fuels</u> are being used faster than they're being replaced — so we'll need <u>alternatives</u>. There are quite a few options (e.g. wind, nuclear, wave, solar, and so on) — they <u>all</u> have pros and cons.

Wind Farms — Lots of Little Wind Turbines

1) Wind power involves putting lots of wind turbines up in <u>exposed places</u> — like on <u>moors</u>, around the <u>coast</u> or <u>out at sea</u>.

2) Wind turbines convert the kinetic energy of moving air into electricity. The <u>wind</u> turns the <u>blades</u>, which turn a <u>generator</u>.

3) Wind turbines are quite cheap to run — they're very <u>tough</u> and reliable, and the wind is <u>free</u>.

4) Even better, wind power doesn't produce any <u>polluting waste</u> and it's <u>renewable</u> — the wind's never going to run out.

5) But there are <u>disadvantages</u>. You need about 1500 wind turbines to replace one coal-fired power station. Some people think that 'wind farms' spoil the view and the spinning blades cause noise pollution.

6) Another problem is that sometimes the wind isn't <u>strong enough</u> to generate any power. It's also impossible to increase supply when there's extra demand (e.g. when Coronation Street starts).

7) And although the wind is free, it's <u>expensive</u> to <u>set up</u> a wind farm, especially <u>out at sea</u>.

Nuclear Power Uses Uranium as Fuel

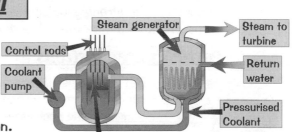

1) A <u>nuclear power station</u> uses <u>uranium</u> to produce <u>heat</u> (which makes <u>steam</u> to drive <u>turbines</u> — see p17).

2) Nuclear power stations are expensive to <u>build</u> and <u>maintain</u>, and they take <u>longer</u> to <u>start up</u> than fossil fuel power stations. (<u>Natural gas</u> is the quickest.)

3) <u>Processing</u> the <u>uranium</u> before you use it causes pollution.

4) And there's always a risk of <u>leaks</u> of radioactive material, or even a <u>major catastrophe</u> like the <u>Chernobyl disaster</u> (which can both cause cancer — see page 56).

5) A big problem with nuclear power is the <u>radioactive waste</u> that you always get — it's very <u>dangerous</u> and difficult to <u>dispose of</u> or reprocess (but see below).

6) And when they're too old and inefficient, nuclear power stations have to be <u>decommissioned</u> (shut down and made safe) — that's expensive too.

7) But there are many <u>advantages</u> to nuclear power. It <u>doesn't</u> produce any of the <u>greenhouse gases</u> which contribute to <u>global warming</u>. Many people think this benefit outweighs its disadvantages.

8) Also, there's still plenty of <u>uranium</u> left in the ground (although it can take a lot of money and energy to make it suitable for use in a reactor).

Nuclear Fuel is Also Used to Make Nuclear Weapons

1) The <u>used</u> uranium fuel rods from nuclear power stations can be <u>reprocessed</u>. This is one way of dealing with some of the radioactive waste that would otherwise have to be <u>stored</u>.

2) After reprocessing, you're left with more uranium and a bit of <u>plutonium</u>.

3) You can <u>reuse</u> the uranium in your nuclear power station.

See page 24 for more about nuclear waste.

4) The <u>plutonium</u> can be used to make <u>nuclear weapons</u>.

I love wind farms — as long as they're organic...

Building loads of nuclear power stations would mean we wouldn't have rely on fossil fuels — and we wouldn't have to buy oil from other countries. The Government thinks we should be getting much of our energy from <u>renewable sources</u> — they want renewable energy to meet 10% of our needs by 2010.

Nuclear Radiation

Sometimes the <u>nucleus</u> of an atom can (for no immediately obvious reason) spit out <u>particles</u> or <u>energy</u>. The stuff that gets spat out is called <u>nuclear radiation</u> — and there are three kinds.

Nuclear Radiation Causes Ionisation

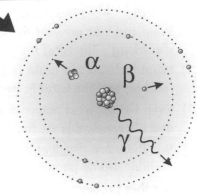

1) When an unstable nucleus <u>decays</u>, it gives off one or more kinds of <u>nuclear radiation</u>.

2) The three kinds of radiation are <u>alpha</u> (α), <u>beta</u> (β) and <u>gamma</u> (γ).

3) All three kinds of radiation can cause <u>ionisation</u> — which means they knock <u>electrons</u> off atoms, turning those atoms into positively charged <u>ions</u>. (The electrons that have been knocked off can then be gained by other atoms, forming negative ions.) This ionisation can cause <u>health problems</u> — see p56.

4) The ionising power of each kind of radiation is linked to how far it can <u>penetrate</u> materials. The <u>further</u> the radiation can penetrate before hitting an atom, the <u>less ionising</u> it is.

Alpha Particles are Big and Heavy

1) <u>Alpha particles</u> (α) are relatively big, heavy and slow moving (they're 2 protons and 2 neutrons).

2) Because of their size they're <u>stopped quickly</u> — they <u>don't penetrate</u> far into materials. Alpha particles can be stopped by <u>paper</u> or <u>skin</u>.

3) This means they're <u>strongly ionising</u> — they bash into loads of atoms and knock electrons off them before they slow down.

Beta Particles are Electrons

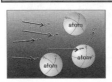

1) <u>Beta particles</u> (β) are just <u>electrons</u> — so they're <u>small</u>, and they move quite <u>fast</u>. (Don't get these beta-radiation electrons confused with the electrons orbiting round the <u>outside</u> of the nucleus — these electrons come from <u>inside the nucleus</u>.)

2) Beta particles <u>penetrate moderately</u> (further than α-particles) before colliding, so they're <u>moderately ionising</u>. But they can still be stopped by a thin sheet of <u>metal</u>.

Gamma Rays are Very High Frequency Electromagnetic Waves

1) After spitting out an α- or β-particle, the nucleus might need to get rid of some extra energy. It does this by emitting a <u>gamma ray</u> (γ) — a type of <u>EM radiation</u>, see p56.

2) Gamma rays have <u>no mass</u> and <u>no charge</u>. They can penetrate a <u>long way</u> into materials without being stopped — meaning they're <u>weakly ionising</u> (they tend to <u>pass through</u> rather than collide with atoms). But eventually they do hit something and do damage.

3) They can be stopped using very <u>thick concrete</u> or <u>thick lead</u>.

Background Radiation is Everywhere All the Time

There's (low-level) <u>background nuclear radiation</u> all around us all the time. It comes from:

1) substances here on <u>Earth</u> — some radioactivity comes from air, food, building materials, soil, rocks...

2) radiation from <u>space</u> (cosmic rays) — these come mostly from the Sun (see p26),

3) <u>living things</u> — there's a little bit of radioactive material in all living things,

4) radiation due to <u>human activity</u> — e.g. fallout from nuclear explosions or nuclear waste (though this is usually a tiny proportion of the total background radiation).

Learn this diagram — it's ace...

You can tell which kind of radiation you're dealing with by what <u>blocks</u> it. If it gets through paper, it could be beta or gamma. If it gets through a thin sheet of aluminium, it <u>must</u> be gamma. I'll make a prediction — I'll bet you get a question on this.

Thin mica | Skin or paper stops ALPHA | Thin aluminium stops BETA | Thick lead stops GAMMA

Uses of Nuclear Radiation

Nuclear radiation can be very <u>dangerous</u>. But it can be very <u>useful</u> too. Read on...

Alpha Radiation is Used in Smoke Detectors

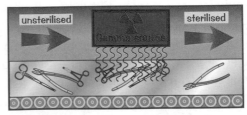

1) Smoke detectors have a <u>weak</u> source of α-radiation close to <u>two electrodes</u>.

2) The radiation <u>ionises</u> the air, and a <u>current</u> flows between the electrodes.

3) But if there's a fire, the <u>smoke</u> <u>absorbs</u> the <u>radiation</u> — the <u>current stops</u> and the <u>alarm sounds</u>.

Beta Radiation is Used in Tracers and Thickness Gauges

1) Radioactive substances have <u>medical</u> uses.

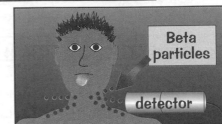

For example, if a radioactive source is <u>injected</u> into a patient (or <u>swallowed</u>), its progress around the body can be followed using an <u>external radiation detector</u>. A computer converts the reading to a TV display showing where the strongest reading is coming from. These '<u>tracers</u>' can show if the body is working properly.

Doctors use <u>beta</u> or <u>gamma</u> emitters as <u>tracers</u> because this radiation <u>passes out</u> of the body. They also choose things that are only radioactive for a <u>few hours</u>.

2) <u>Beta-radiation</u> is also used in <u>thickness control</u>. You direct radiation through the stuff being made (e.g. paper or cardboard), and put a detector on the other side, connected to a control unit.

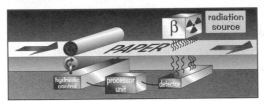

When the amount of <u>detected</u> radiation goes <u>down</u>, it means the paper is coming out <u>too thick</u>, so the control unit pinches the rollers up a bit to make it thinner.

If the reading goes <u>up</u>, the paper's <u>too thin</u>, so the control unit opens the rollers out a bit.

For this use, your radioactive substance mustn't decay away <u>too quickly</u>, otherwise its strength would gradually fall (and the control unit would keep pinching up the rollers trying to compensate).

You need to use a <u>beta</u> source, because then the paper or cardboard will <u>partly block</u> the radiation. If it <u>all</u> goes through (or <u>none</u> of it does), then the reading <u>won't change</u> at all as the thickness changes.

Gamma Radiation Has Medical and Industrial Uses

1) High doses of <u>gamma rays</u> will kill <u>all</u> living cells, so they can be used to treat <u>cancers</u>.

The gamma rays have to be <u>directed carefully</u> at the cancer, and at just the right <u>dosage</u> so as to kill the <u>cancer</u> cells <u>without</u> damaging too many <u>normal</u> cells.

2) Gamma rays are also used to <u>sterilise</u> medical instruments — by <u>killing</u> all the microbes.

This is better than trying to <u>boil</u> plastic instruments, which might be damaged by high temperatures. You need to use a strongly radioactive source that lasts a long time, so that it doesn't need replacing too often.

3) Several industries also use gamma radiation to do <u>non-destructive testing</u>. For example, <u>airlines</u> can check the turbine blades of their jet engines by directing gamma rays at them — if too much radiation <u>gets through</u> the blade to the <u>detector</u> on the other side, they know the blade's <u>cracked</u> or there's a fault in the welding. It's so much better to find this out before you take off than in mid-air.

Thickness gauges — they're called 'exams' nowadays...

Knowing the detail is important here. For instance, swallowing an alpha source as a medical tracer would be very foolish — alpha radiation would cause all sorts of chaos inside your body but couldn't be detected outside, making the whole thing pointless. So learn <u>what</u> each type's used for <u>and why</u>.

Danger from Radioactive Materials

Radioactive stuff certainly has its uses — curing cancer, killing bacteria and so on.
But if you don't want to <u>irradiate yourself</u>, you have to know how to handle it safely.

You Should Always Protect Yourself...

1) First things first... don't do anything <u>really</u> stupid — like <u>eating</u> your smoke alarm.

2) Radioactive sources need to be <u>stored</u> safely. They should be kept in a <u>labelled</u> <u>lead box</u> and put back in as soon you can to keep your <u>exposure time</u> short.

3) If you need to use a radioactive source, always handle it with <u>tongs</u> — <u>never</u> allow <u>skin contact</u>. And keep it at <u>arm's length</u> (so it's as <u>far</u> from the body as possible). Also, keep it pointing <u>away</u> from you and avoid <u>looking</u> directly at it.

...Especially If You Work with Nuclear Radiation

1) Industrial nuclear workers wear <u>full protective suits</u> to prevent <u>tiny radioactive</u> <u>particles</u> being <u>inhaled</u>, or lodging <u>on the skin</u> or <u>under fingernails</u>, etc.

2) <u>Lead-lined suits</u> and <u>lead/concrete barriers</u> and <u>thick lead screens</u> shield workers from <u>gamma rays</u> in highly contaminated areas. (α- and β-radiation is stopped much more easily.)

3) Workers use <u>remote-controlled robot arms</u> to carry out tasks in highly radioactive areas.

Radioactive Waste is Difficult to Dispose of Safely

1) Most waste from nuclear power stations and hospitals is '<u>low-level</u>' (only slightly radioactive). Low-level waste is things like paper, clothing, gloves, syringes, etc. This kind of waste can be disposed of by <u>burying</u> it in secure landfill sites.

2) <u>High-level</u> waste is the really dangerous stuff — a lot of it stays highly radioactive for <u>tens of</u> <u>thousands</u> of years, and so has to be treated very carefully. It's often sealed into <u>glass blocks</u>, which are then sealed in <u>metal canisters</u>. These <u>could</u> then be buried <u>deep</u> underground.

3) However, it's difficult to find <u>suitable places</u> to bury high-level waste. The site has to be <u>geologically</u> <u>stable</u> (e.g. not suffer from earthquakes), since big movements in the rock could disturb the canisters and allow radioactive material to <u>leak out</u>. If this material gets into the <u>groundwater</u>, it could contaminate the soil, plants, rivers, etc., and get into our <u>drinking water</u>.

4) Even when geologists <u>do</u> find suitable sites, people who live nearby often object. So, at the moment, most high level waste is kept 'on-site' at nuclear power stations.

5) Not <u>all</u> radioactive waste has to be chucked out though — some of it is <u>reprocessed</u> to reclaim useful radioactive material. But even reprocessing leaves some waste behind.

6) Nuclear power stations and reprocessing plants are generally pretty <u>secure</u> — they have high fences and security checks on the people going in and out. But they might still be a target for <u>terrorists</u> — who could use <u>stolen</u> radioactive material to make a 'dirty bomb', or <u>attack</u> the plant directly.

7) There are strict regulations about how waste is disposed of. But the rules could <u>change</u> as we find out more about the dangers of radiation, and the pros and cons of storing waste in different ways. What's allowed now might be considered too risky in the future.

Radioactive sources — don't put them on your chips...

Most of the UK's nuclear power stations are quite old, and will have to be shut down soon. There's a debate going on over whether we should build <u>new ones</u>. Some people say no — if we can't deal safely with the radioactive waste we've got <u>now</u>, we certainly shouldn't make lots <u>more</u>. Others say that nuclear power is the only way to meet all our energy needs without causing catastrophic <u>climate change</u>.

Earth's Magnetic Field

Compasses always point north. Not the compasses you draw <u>circles</u> with, obviously — they point wherever you point them. The <u>really useful</u> kind of compass, when you're lost, is the <u>magnetic</u> kind.

The Earth is a Bit Like a Big Magnet

1) The Earth is surrounded by a <u>magnetic field</u> — a region where <u>magnetic materials</u> (like iron and steel) experience a <u>force</u>.
Basically, this means the Earth acts like a big <u>bar magnet</u>.

2) Like all magnets, it has <u>north</u> and <u>south poles</u>.
But... (concentrate now) the Earth's <u>south magnetic pole</u> is actually at the <u>North Pole</u>.
This makes sense if you think about it... if you have a <u>compass</u> (or any other magnet), its north pole <u>points north</u> — because it's attracted towards a <u>south magnetic pole</u> (remember, opposites attract).

3) You can use a compass to tell the direction of the magnetic field. The needle points in the direction of the field.

The Earth's Molten Iron Core Causes Its Magnetic Field

1) The Earth <u>doesn't</u> actually have a <u>giant bar magnet</u> buried inside it. Its <u>core</u> contains a lot of <u>molten iron</u> which moves in <u>convection currents</u> (see p3). Scientists don't understand this fully, but they think that <u>electric currents</u> within this <u>liquid core</u> create the <u>magnetic field</u> (and vice versa).

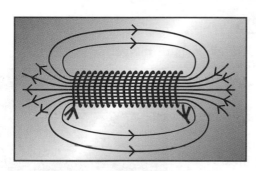

2) In fact, <u>magnetic fields</u> are generated whenever <u>charged particles</u> are <u>moving around</u>.
This means you get a magnetic field whenever <u>electricity</u> flows (since electricity is a flow of electrons).

3) So if you take a coil of wire and let an <u>electrical current</u> flow through it, you'll get a <u>magnetic field</u>.
And the shape of this magnetic field will be pretty similar to the shape of the Earth's magnetic field. (Plus you get a strong magnetic field <u>inside</u> the coil.)

The Moon May Have Come from a Colliding Planet

Scientists can use what they know about the Earth and the Moon to come up with believable theories about where the Moon came from in the first place. It's pretty amazing.

1) Scientists think that 'our' Moon was formed when <u>another planet</u> collided side-on with Earth.

2) The theory is that some time after the Earth was formed, a smaller Mars-sized object <u>crashed into it</u>. In the heat of the collision, the <u>dense iron cores</u> of these two planets <u>merged</u> to form the <u>Earth</u>'s core.

3) The <u>less dense</u> material was <u>ejected</u> as really hot dust and rocks — which orbited around the Earth for a while and eventually came together to form the <u>Moon</u>.

4) There's quite a bit of <u>evidence</u> for this theory. For example...

- The Moon has a <u>lower density</u> than the Earth and <u>doesn't</u> have a big iron core, whereas Earth does.
- Moon rocks contain few substances which evaporate at low temperatures — suggesting that the Moon formed from <u>hot</u> material (all the water, etc. was boiled away, as would happen in a collision).

So my compass points north — which is the south pole, you say...

I'm not saying that this is the <u>easiest</u> stuff in the world to get your head round. But it's kind of interesting. I mean... you can look up at the Moon and <u>wonder</u> at the events of the past. <u>Amazing</u>. Any road up... learn the stuff on this page (and all the others), and you'll be <u>fine</u> come exam day.

Particles and Rays from the Sun

The Sun's pretty important for life on Earth. Without its light and heat, I reckon it'd probably be a bit dark and a bit nippy. But the Sun also emits very <u>weird stuff</u>, like <u>cosmic rays</u> and <u>solar flares</u>.

Earth's Magnetic Field Shields Us from Charged Particles

1) The surface of the Sun is a very unpleasant place — the Sun's constantly releasing enormous amounts of <u>energy</u> and <u>cosmic rays</u>. Cosmic rays are heavily <u>ionising</u>, and mostly consist of <u>charged particles</u>, though there's gamma rays and X-rays in there too. (Cosmic rays are given off by other things in space as well, but most of those that hit the Earth come from <u>the Sun</u>.)

2) The Earth's magnetic field does a good job of <u>shielding</u> us from a lot of the charged particles from the Sun by deflecting them away.

DETLEV VAN RAVENSWAAY/
SCIENCE PHOTO LIBRARY

3) But when the charged particles in <u>cosmic rays</u> hit the Earth's atmosphere they create <u>gamma rays</u> (which form part of the Earth's natural background radiation — see page 22).

4) From time to time, massive <u>explosions</u> called <u>solar flares</u> also occur on the surface of the Sun. Solar flares release <u>vast</u> amounts of energy. Some of this energy is given off as <u>gamma rays</u> and <u>X-rays</u> — both potentially harmful to us here on Earth.

5) Solar flares also give off <u>massive</u> clouds of <u>charged particles</u> — these are ejected at very <u>high speeds</u>. Some reach the Earth and produce <u>disturbances</u> in the Earth's <u>magnetic field</u>.

Solar Flares Cause All Sorts of Problems

1) Solar flares can damage <u>artificial satellites</u>, which we rely on for <u>all sorts</u> of things:
   - modern <u>communications</u>,
   - studying the <u>weather</u> to make <u>forecasts</u>,
   - <u>spying</u>,
   - <u>navigation</u> systems (such as GPS).

2) The problem is that <u>electrons</u> and <u>ions</u> in solar flares can cause <u>surges</u> of <u>current</u> in a satellite's electrical circuitry. So satellites might need to be <u>shut down</u> to prevent damage during flares.

3) Solar flares also interact with the Earth's magnetic field, and can cause <u>power surges</u> in electricity distribution systems here on Earth (by means of <u>electromagnetic induction</u> — see p88). In 1989, a solar flare disrupted electricity supplies for 6 million people in Quebec, in Canada.

Cosmic Rays Cause the Aurora Borealis

1) Some charged particles in cosmic rays are <u>deflected</u> by the Earth's magnetic field and spiral down near the <u>magnetic poles</u>. Here, some of their <u>energy</u> is transferred to particles in the Earth's atmosphere, causing them to emit light — the <u>polar lights</u>.

2) The polar lights are shifting 'curtains' of light that appear in the sky. They're called the aurora borealis (<u>northern lights</u>) at the North Pole and the aurora australis at the South Pole. These displays are more dramatic during solar flares, when more cosmic rays arrive at the Earth.

Solar flares — they were big in the seventies...

In an old Scandinavian language, the word for 'northern lights' is 'herring flash' — people used to think the lights were <u>reflections</u> cast into the sky by large shoals of <u>herring</u>. That's not an <u>entirely</u> stupid idea, but <u>not</u> what you call the <u>accepted explanation</u> nowadays — so don't try it in the exam.

The Solar System

My primary school teacher, Mrs Evans, told me there were <u>nine planets</u> out there. But scientists have decided that Pluto doesn't count as a planet. Poor Pluto. Still, at least it's one less for you to learn.

Planets Reflect Sunlight and Orbit the Sun in Ellipses

Our solar system consists of a <u>star</u> (<u>the Sun</u>) and lots of stuff <u>orbiting</u> it in <u>slightly elongated</u> circles (called ellipses).

- Closest to the Sun are the <u>inner planets</u> — Mercury, Venus, Earth and Mars.
- Then the <u>asteroid belt</u> — see p28.
- Then the <u>outer planets</u>, much further away — Jupiter, Saturn, Uranus, Neptune.

You need to learn the <u>order</u> of the planets, which is made easier by using the little jollyism below:

Mercury, Venus, Earth, Mars, (Asteroids), Jupiter, Saturn, Uranus, Neptune
(Mad Vampires Eat Mangoes And Jump Straight Up Noses)

1) You can <u>see</u> some planets with the <u>naked eye</u>. They look like <u>stars</u>, but they're <u>totally different</u>.

2) Stars are <u>huge</u>, very <u>hot</u> and very <u>far away</u>. They <u>give out</u> lots of <u>light</u> — which is why you can see them, even though they're very far away.

3) The planets are <u>smaller</u> and <u>nearer</u> and they just <u>reflect sunlight</u> falling on them.

4) Planets often have <u>moons</u> orbiting around them. Jupiter has at least 63 of 'em. We've just got one (see p25 for more about our Moon).

The Solar System is Held Together by Gravity

1) Things only <u>change direction</u> when a <u>force</u> acts on them — if there were no force, they'd move in a straight line (or stay still). Since planets go round and round, there must be a force involved.

2) When it comes to <u>big</u> things in the Solar System and the rest of the Universe (like planets, asteroids, comets, meteors, and so on), there's only really one force it could be — <u>gravity</u>.

3) Gravity pulls <u>everything</u> in the Universe towards <u>everything else</u>. The effect is tiny between 'small' things (e.g. between you and a car, or between a house and a hat) — so tiny you don't notice it. But when you're talking about things as heavy as <u>stars</u> and <u>planets</u>, the pull of gravity can be <u>huge</u> (the bigger the 'thing', the bigger its pull). So it's <u>gravity</u> that makes planets orbit stars, and moons orbit planets. <u>Gravity</u> keeps satellites, comets and asteroids in their orbits, and so on. Get the idea...

4) But the pull of an object gets <u>smaller</u> the <u>further away</u> you go. This is why you're pulled strongly towards the Earth and don't hurtle towards the Sun, for example. And this is why the Earth orbits the Sun, rather than some other much bigger star further away.

The pull of gravity is <u>directly</u> towards the Sun...

...but the motion of the Earth is <u>around</u> the Sun.

There's a bit more on this in Module P5 — see page 65.

5) If the Earth wasn't <u>already</u> moving, it would be pulled by gravity <u>directly towards</u> the Sun. But what gravity normally does is make things that are already moving change their course — often into <u>circular</u> or elliptical <u>orbits</u>.

- <u>Circular motion</u> is always caused by a <u>force</u> (pull) towards the <u>centre</u> of the circle. For planets, moons, etc. in an orbit, this force is provided by <u>gravity</u>.
- A force that causes a circular motion is called a <u>centripetal force</u>.

Pull yourself together — get this stuff learnt...

Gravity's a pretty amazing force. Not only does it keep your feet on the ground (ho ho) but without it, there wouldnt' be a ground to keep your feet on. IT was gravity that pulled together lots of little bits of gas and dust and eventually formed the Earth. Cheers gravity, you did a grand job...

Asteroids and Comets

As you read this, there are thousands of hefty lumps of rock just <u>whizzing about</u> in space — and one of them might be coming <u>straight at you</u>.

There's a Belt of Asteroids Orbiting Between Mars and Jupiter

1) When the Solar System was forming, the rocks between Mars and Jupiter didn't form a planet — the large <u>gravitational force</u> of Jupiter kept interfering.

2) This left millions of <u>asteroids</u> — <u>piles of rubble and rock</u> measuring 1 km to about 1000 km in diameter. They orbit the Sun between the orbits of <u>Jupiter</u> and <u>Mars</u>.

3) Asteroids usually <u>stay in their orbits</u> but sometimes they're <u>pushed</u> or <u>pulled</u> into different ones...

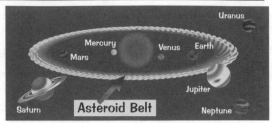
Asteroid Belt
Not to scale.

Meteorites are Rocks That Have Crashed Down to Earth

1) <u>Meteors</u> are rocks or dust that enter the Earth's atmosphere. As they pass through the <u>atmosphere</u> they <u>burn up</u>, and we see them as '<u>shooting stars</u>'.

2) Sometimes, not all of the meteor burns up and part of it crashes into the <u>Earth's surface</u> as a <u>meteorite</u>. This only happens <u>rarely</u>, but when large meteors do hit us, they can cause <u>havoc</u>...

3) They can start <u>fires</u>, and throw loads of <u>hot rocks</u> and <u>dust</u> into the air. They also make big <u>holes</u> in the ground (<u>craters</u>, if we're being technical).

4) The <u>dust</u> and <u>smoke</u> from a large impact can <u>block out</u> the <u>sunlight</u> for many months, causing <u>climate change</u> — which in turn can cause <u>species</u> to become <u>extinct</u>. About 65 million years ago an asteroid about <u>10 km across</u> struck the <u>Yucatán peninsula</u> in Mexico. The dust it kicked up caused global temperatures to plummet, and over half the species on Earth subsequently died out (including maybe the last of the <u>dinosaurs</u>).

Meteorite hit about here...

5) We can tell that asteroids have collided with Earth in the past. There are the <u>big craters</u>, but also:
   • layers of <u>unusual elements</u> in rocks — these must have been 'imported' by an asteroid,
   • sudden changes in <u>fossil numbers</u> between adjacent layers of rock, as species suffer extinction.

Comets Orbit the Sun in Very Elliptical Orbits

1) <u>Comets</u> are balls of <u>rock</u>, <u>dust</u> and <u>ice</u> which orbit the Sun in very <u>elongated</u> ellipses, often in different planes from the planets. The Sun is near one end of the orbit.

2) As a comet approaches the Sun, its ice <u>melts</u>, leaving a bright <u>tail</u> of gas and debris which can be millions of kilometres long. This is what we see from the Earth.

3) Comets <u>speed up</u> as they approach the Sun, because of the pull of the Sun's <u>gravity</u>. (And this pull gets really strong close to the Sun.)

Comet

Near-Earth Objects (NEOs) Could Collide with Earth

1) Near-Earth objects (NEOs) are <u>asteroids</u> or <u>comets</u> which might be on a <u>collision course</u> with Earth.

2) Astronomers use <u>powerful telescopes</u> and <u>satellites</u> to search for and monitor NEOs. Then they can calculate an object's <u>trajectory</u> (the path it's going to take) and find out if it's heading for <u>us</u>.

3) <u>If</u> we get enough warning, we could try to <u>deflect</u> an NEO before it hits us. Scientists have various ideas about this — you could explode a nuclear bomb next to the object to 'nudge' it off course, or you could speed it up (or slow it down) so that it reaches Earth's orbit when we're out of the way.

Asteroids... my dad had those — very nasty...

It's serious business, this NEO stuff. In 2002, an asteroid narrowly missed us, and we only found it <u>12 days</u> beforehand — not very much time to put a plan together. Even if Bruce Willis had been on hand.

Beyond the Solar System

There's all sorts of exciting stuff out there... Our whole Solar System is just part of a huge <u>galaxy</u>.
And there are billions upon billions of galaxies. You should be realising now that the Universe is huge...

We're in the Milky Way Galaxy

1) Our <u>Sun</u> is just one of <u>many billions</u> of <u>stars</u> which form
the <u>Milky Way galaxy</u>. Our Sun is about halfway along
one of the <u>spiral arms</u> of the Milky Way.

2) The <u>distance</u> between neighbouring stars in the galaxy is
usually <u>millions of times greater</u> than the distance
between <u>planets</u> in our Solar System.

3) The <u>force</u> which keeps the stars together in a galaxy is
<u>gravity</u>, of course. And like most things in the Universe,
galaxies <u>rotate</u> — a bit like a Catherine wheel.

You are here

You are here

The Whole Universe Has More Than a Billion Galaxies

1) Galaxies themselves are often <u>millions of times</u> further
apart than the stars are within a galaxy.

2) So even the slowest among you will have worked out that
the Universe is <u>mostly empty space</u> and is <u>really really BIG</u>.

Scientists Measure Distances in Space Using Light Years

1) Once you get outside our Solar System, the distances between stars and between galaxies are <u>so
enormous</u> that kilometres seem <u>pathetically small</u> for measuring them.

2) For example, the <u>closest</u> star to us (after the Sun) is about 40 000 000 000 000 kilometres away
(give or take a few hundred billion kilometres). Numbers like that soon get out of hand.

3) So scientists use <u>light years</u> instead — a <u>light year</u> is the <u>distance</u> that <u>light travels</u> through a vacuum
(like space) in one <u>year</u>. Simple as that.

4) If you work it out, 1 light year is equal to about 9 460 000 000 000 kilometres.
Which means the closest star after the Sun is about <u>4.2 light years</u> away from us.

5) Just remember — a light year is a measure of <u>DISTANCE</u> (<u>not</u> time).

Stars Can Explode — and They Sometimes Leave Black Holes

1) When a <u>really big</u> star has used up all its fuel, it <u>explodes</u>. What's left after
the explosion is really <u>dense</u> — sometimes so dense that <u>nothing</u> can
escape its gravitational pull. It's now called a <u>black hole</u>.

See page 32 for more
about the death of stars.

2) Black holes have a very <u>large mass</u> but their diameter is <u>tiny</u> in comparison.

3) They're <u>not visible</u> — even <u>light</u> can't escape their gravitational pull (that's why it's 'black', d'oh).

4) Astronomers have to detect black holes in other ways — e.g. they can observe <u>X-rays</u> emitted by
<u>hot gases</u> from other stars as they spiral into the black hole.

Spiral arms — would you still need elbows...

A lot of people say it's a small world. I'm not sure... it's always seemed pretty big to me.
Anyway... you <u>never</u> hear <u>anybody</u> say the Universe is small. Not nowadays, anyway. Weirdly though,
the Universe used to be <u>tiny</u> (see page 31). That was a while ago now though. Before my time.

Exploring the Solar System

If you want to know what it's like on another planet, you have three options — peer at it from a distance, send a robot to have a peek, or get in a spaceship and go there yourself...

We Can Explore Space Using Manned Spacecraft...

1) The Solar System is <u>big</u> — so big that even radio waves (which travel at 300 000 000 m/s) take several <u>hours</u> to cross it. Even from <u>Mars</u>, radio signals take at least a couple of <u>minutes</u>.

2) But sending a <u>manned spacecraft</u> to Mars would take at least a couple of <u>years</u> (for a round trip).

3) The spacecraft would need to carry a lot of <u>fuel</u>, making it <u>heavy</u> — and <u>expensive</u>.

4) And it would be difficult keeping the astronauts <u>alive</u> and <u>healthy</u> for all that time...
   - the spacecraft would have to carry loads of <u>food</u>, <u>water</u> and <u>oxygen</u> (or be <u>very good</u> at <u>recycling</u> them),
   - you'd need to regulate the <u>temperature</u> and remove <u>toxic gases</u> (e.g. CO_2) from the air,
   - the spacecraft would have to <u>shield</u> the astronauts from <u>cosmic rays</u> (see p26),
   - long periods in <u>low gravity</u> causes <u>muscle wastage</u> and loss of <u>bone tissue</u>,
   - spending <u>ages</u> in a <u>tiny space</u>, with the <u>same people</u>, is psychologically <u>stressful</u>.

Space travel can be very stressful.

...but Sending Unmanned Probes is Much Easier

First, build a <u>spacecraft</u>. Then build and program loads of <u>instruments</u> — to <u>record data</u> and <u>send it back</u> to Earth (probably by radio). Finish the job by packing the instruments on board, turning on the computer and launching your probe. Like I said... easy.

1) '<u>Fly-by</u>' missions are simplest — the probe passes close by an object but doesn't land. It can gather data on loads of things, including <u>temperature</u>, <u>magnetic and gravitational fields</u> and <u>radiation levels</u>.

2) Sometimes a probe is programmed to enter a planet's <u>atmosphere</u>. It might be designed to <u>burn up</u> after a while, having already sent back lots of data — about the atmosphere and radiation levels, say.

3) Some probes are designed to <u>land</u> on other planets (or moons, asteroids...). They often carry exploration <u>rovers</u> that can <u>wander</u> about, taking photos, etc. On Mars recently, NASA's two rovers (called 'Spirit' and 'Opportunity') were able to search for features of interest, e.g. evidence of water.

Advantages of Unmanned Probes

- They don't have to carry <u>food</u>, <u>water</u> and <u>oxygen</u>.
- They can withstand conditions that would be <u>lethal</u> to humans (e.g. extreme heat, cold or radiation levels).
- With no people taking up room and weighing the probe down, more <u>instruments</u> can be fitted in.
- They're <u>cheaper</u> — they carry less, they don't have to come back to Earth, and less is spent on <u>safety</u>.
- If the probe does crash or burn up unexpectedly it's a bit <u>embarrassing</u>, and you've wasted lots of time and money, but at least <u>no one gets hurt</u>.

Disadvantages of Unmanned Probes

- Unmanned probes can't <u>think for themselves</u> (whereas people are very good at overcoming simple problems that could be disastrous).
- A spacecraft can't do maintenance and <u>repairs</u> — people can (as the astronauts on the Space Shuttle 'Discovery' had to do when its heat shield was damaged during take-off).

Probes — a popular feature of alien abduction stories...

When people first sent things into space, we began cautiously — in October 1957, Russia sent a small aluminium sphere (Sputnik 1) into orbit around the Earth. A month later, off went Sputnik 2, carrying the very first earthling to leave the planet — a small and unfortunate <u>dog</u> called Laika.

The Origin of the Universe

How did it all begin... Well, once upon a time, there was a really <u>Big Bang</u>.
(That's the <u>most convincing theory</u> we've got for how the Universe started.)

The Universe Seems to be Expanding

As big as the Universe already is, it looks like it's getting even bigger.
All its <u>galaxies</u> seem to be moving away from each other. There's good evidence for this...

Light from Distant Galaxies is Red-Shifted

1) When we look at <u>light from distant galaxies</u> we find that the <u>frequencies</u>
   are all <u>lower</u> than they should be — they're <u>shifted</u> towards the <u>red end</u>
   of the spectrum.

2) This <u>red-shift</u> is the same effect as a car <u>horn</u> sounding lower-pitched
   when the car is travelling <u>away</u> from you. The sound <u>drops in frequency</u>.

3) <u>Measurements</u> of the red-shift suggest that <u>all the distant galaxies</u> are
   <u>moving away from us</u> very quickly — and it's the <u>same result</u> whichever
   direction you look in.

More Distant Galaxies Have Greater Red-Shifts

1) <u>More distant</u> galaxies have <u>greater</u> red-shifts than nearer ones.

2) This means that more distant galaxies are <u>moving away faster</u> than nearer ones.
   The inescapable <u>conclusion</u> appears to be that the whole Universe is <u>expanding</u>.

There's Microwave Radiation from All Directions

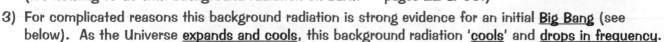

This is another observation that scientists made. It's not interesting in
itself, but the theory that explains all this evidence definitely is.

1) Scientists can detect <u>low frequency radiation</u> coming
   from <u>all directions</u> and <u>all parts</u> of the Universe.

2) It's known as the <u>cosmic background radiation</u>.
   (It's nothing to do with background radiation on Earth — pages 22 & 59.)

3) For complicated reasons this background radiation is strong evidence for an initial <u>Big Bang</u> (see
   below). As the Universe <u>expands and cools</u>, this background radiation '<u>cools</u>' and <u>drops in frequency</u>.

This Evidence Suggests the Universe Started with a Bang

So all the galaxies are moving away from each other at great speed — suggesting something must have
<u>got them going</u>. That 'something' was probably a <u>big explosion</u> — the <u>Big Bang</u>. Here's the theory...

1) Initially, all the matter in the Universe occupied <u>a very small space</u> (that's
   <u>all</u> the matter in <u>all</u> the galaxies squashed into a space <u>much much smaller</u>
   than a pin-head — <u>wowzers</u>). Then it '<u>exploded</u>' — the space started
   expanding, and the <u>expansion</u> is still going on.

2) The Big Bang theory lets us guess the <u>age</u> of the Universe.
   From the current <u>rate of expansion</u>, we think the Universe is about
   <u>14 billion years</u> old.

3) But estimates of the age of the Universe are <u>very difficult</u> because it's hard
   to tell how much the expansion has <u>slowed down</u> since the Big Bang.

<u>In the beginning, there were — no exams...</u>

'How it all began' is quite a tricky problem. Some religious people say that God created the world.
Among scientists, the theory of a 'big bang' to get things started is now generally accepted, because
that's what the <u>evidence</u> suggests. But we're still rather hazy about if/when/how it's all going to end...

The Life Cycle of Stars

Stars go through many traumatic stages in their lives — just like teenagers.

Clouds of Dust and Gas

1) Stars initially form from clouds of DUST AND GAS.

Protostar

2) The force of gravity makes the gas and dust spiral in together to form a protostar. Gravitational energy has been converted into heat energy, so the temperature rises.

3) When the temperature gets high enough, hydrogen nuclei undergo thermonuclear fusion to form helium nuclei and give out massive amounts of heat and light. A star is born. It immediately enters a long stable period where the heat created by the nuclear fusion provides an outward pressure to balance the force of gravity pulling everything inwards. In this stable period it's called a **MAIN SEQUENCE STAR** and it lasts several billion years. (The Sun is in the middle of this stable period — or to put it another way, the Earth has already had half its innings before the Sun engulfs it!)

Main Sequence Star

4) Eventually the hydrogen begins to run out and the star then swells into a **RED GIANT** (it becomes red because the surface cools).

Red Giant

Small stars

Big stars

5) A small-to-medium-sized star like the Sun then becomes unstable and ejects its outer layer of dust and gas as a planetary nebula.

planetary nebula.... and a White Dwarf

6) This leaves behind a hot, dense solid core — a **WHITE DWARF**, which just cools down and eventually disappears. (That's going to be really sad.)

Neutron Star...

...or Black Hole

Supernova

7) Big stars, however, start to glow brightly again as they undergo more fusion and expand and contract several times, forming heavier elements in various nuclear reactions. Eventually they'll explode in a **SUPERNOVA**.

8) The exploding supernova throws the outer layers of dust and gas into space, leaving a very dense core called a **NEUTRON STAR**. If the star is big enough this will become a **BLACK HOLE** (see p29).

Red Giants, White Dwarfs, Black Holes, Green Ghosts...

Erm. Now how do they know that exactly... Anyway, now you know what the future holds — our Sun is going to fizzle out, and it'll just get **very very cold** and **very very dark**. Great. On a brighter note, the Sun's got a good few years in it yet, so it's still worth passing those exams.

Revision Summary for Module P2

Just what you were waiting for — a whole list of lovely questions to try. You know the routine by now... try the questions, then look back and see what you got right and what you got wrong. If you did get any wrong, you're not ready for the exam — so do more revision and then try the questions again.

1) Give two advantages and one disadvantage of using solar cells to generate electricity.

2) How do solar ovens focus the Sun's rays?

3) Sketch a typical power station, and explain what happens at each stage.

4) Give one advantage and one disadvantage of using: a) fossil fuels; b) biomass, to generate power.

5) Define electromagnetic induction. What factors affect the size of the induced voltage?

6) Describe how a generator works.

7) Explain why a very high electrical voltage is used to transmit electricity in the National Grid.

8) What's the name of the type of transformer that increases voltage? Where are these used?

9) Write down the formula for calculating efficiency.

10)* a) How many units of electricity (in kWh) would a kettle of power 2500 W use in 2 minutes?
    b) How much would that cost, if one unit of electricity costs 12p?

11) Describe how using storage heaters and off-peak electricity could save you money.

12) Explain how wind turbines convert energy from the Sun into electricity.

13) Outline two arguments for and two arguments against increasing the use, in the UK, of
    a) wind power,   b) nuclear power.

14) Describe the nature and ionising power of the three types of radiation: α, β and γ:

15) What substances could be used to block: a) α-radiation   b) β-radiation   c) γ-radiation?

16) List three sources of background radiation.

17) Explain which types of radiation are used, and why, in each of the following:
    a) medical tracers,   b) treating cancer,   c) detecting faults in aeroengine turbine blades,
    d) sterilisation,   e) smoke detectors,   f) thickness control.

18) Describe the precautions you should take when handling radioactive sources in the laboratory.

19) Give examples of radioactive waste which could be disposed of in a secure landfill site.

20) Explain why it's difficult to dispose of high-level radioactive waste safely.

21) Sketch the magnetic fields of: a) the Earth,   b) a coil of wire carrying a current.

22) What do scientists think causes the Earth's magnetic field?

23) Why do scientists think that the Moon may be the result of another planet colliding with Earth?

24) Explain how solar flares can damage an artificial satellite.

25) What causes the northern (and southern) lights? Why does this only occur near the two poles?

26) What force keeps planets and satellites in their orbits?

27) What and where are asteroids? What and where are meteorites? Is there a difference?

28) What and where are comets? What are they made of? Sketch a diagram of a comet orbit.

29) What's a light year?

30) a) Describe the problems with sending a group of astronauts to Neptune.

    b) How else could scientists investigate Neptune's atmosphere, and whether it has a magnetic field?

31) Give two advantages and two disadvantages of manned space travel over unmanned probes.

32) Describe the 'Big Bang' theory for the origin of the Universe. What evidence is there for this theory?

33) Describe the steps that lead to the formation of a main sequence star (like our Sun).

34) What happens inside a star to make it so hot?

35) How are 'black holes' formed from stars? Why are they called 'black'?

36) Why will our Sun never form a black hole?

* Answers on page 100.

Speed and Acceleration

Speed is Just the Distance Travelled in a Certain Time

1) To find the <u>speed</u> of an object, you need to <u>measure</u> the <u>distance</u> it travels (in metres) and the <u>time</u> it takes (in seconds). Then the speed is calculated in <u>metres per second</u> (m/s).

2) You really ought to get <u>pretty slick</u> with this <u>very easy formula</u>:

If the speed isn't constant, this equation gives the <u>average</u> speed.

$$\text{Speed} = \frac{\text{Distance}}{\text{Time}}$$

As usual the <u>formula triangle</u> version makes it all a bit of a <u>breeze</u>.
You just need to try and think up some interesting word for remembering the <u>order</u> of the <u>letters</u> in the triangle, s^dt. Errm... sedit, perhaps... well, I'm sure you can think up something better...

EXAMPLE: A cat skulks 20 metres in 35 seconds.
Find: a) its speed, b) how long it will take to skulk 75 m.
ANSWER: Using the formula triangle: a) s = d/t = 20/35 = 0.5714 = <u>0.57 m/s</u>
b) t = d/s = 75/0.5714 = 131 s = <u>2 min 11 s</u>

Speed Cameras Measure the Speed of Cars

1) <u>Speed cameras</u> can be used to catch speeding motorists at <u>dangerous accident spots</u>.

2) <u>Lines</u> are painted on the road at a <u>certain distance apart</u> to <u>measure</u> the distance travelled by the car.

3) A <u>photo</u> of the car is taken as it passes the first line and a <u>second photo</u> is taken a <u>certain time later</u>.

4) These photos can then be used to measure the <u>distance travelled</u> by the car in this time.

Example: a speed camera takes two photos of a car. The photos are taken <u>0.5 s</u> apart and from the marked lines on the road the distance it travels is measured as <u>5 m</u>. What is the speed of the car?

Answer: Speed = $\frac{\text{distance}}{\text{time}}$ = $\frac{5 \text{ m}}{0.5 \text{ s}}$ = 10 m/s

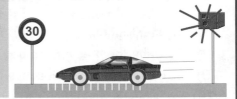

Distance-Time Graphs

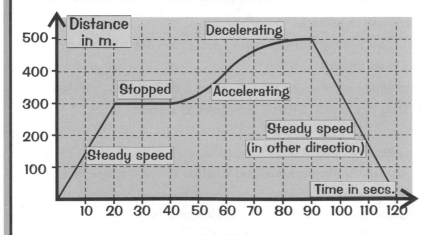

Very Important Notes:

1) <u>GRADIENT</u> = <u>SPEED</u>.

2) <u>Flat sections</u> are where it's <u>stopped</u>.

3) The <u>steeper</u> the graph, the <u>faster</u> it's going.

4) '<u>Downhill</u>' sections mean it's <u>coming back</u> toward its starting point.

5) <u>Curves</u> represent <u>acceleration</u> or deceleration.

6) A <u>steepening curve</u> means it's <u>speeding up</u> (increasing gradient).

7) A <u>levelling off curve</u> means it's <u>slowing down</u> (decreasing gradient).

Calculating Speed from a Distance-Time Graph — It's Just the Gradient

For example the <u>speed</u> of the <u>return section</u> of the graph is:

<u>Speed</u> = gradient = $\frac{\text{vertical}}{\text{horizontal}}$ = $\frac{500}{30}$ = <u>16.7 m/s</u>

Don't forget that you have to use the <u>scales of the axes</u> to work out the gradient. <u>Don't measure in cm</u>.

Speed and Acceleration

Acceleration is How Quickly You're Speeding Up

Acceleration is <u>definitely not</u> the same as <u>speed</u>.
1) Acceleration is <u>how quickly</u> the speed is <u>changing</u>.
2) You also accelerate when you <u>CHANGE DIRECTION</u> <u>without changing speed</u>. (You just need to remember this bit of the definition — you won't have to use it to do any calculations.)
Speed is a simple idea. Acceleration is altogether more <u>subtle</u>, which is why it's <u>confusing</u>.

Acceleration — The Formula:

$$\text{Acceleration} = \frac{\text{Change in Speed}}{\text{Time Taken}}$$

(More on this in P5.)

Well, it's <u>just another formula</u>. Just like all the others. Three things in a <u>formula triangle</u>.
Mind you, there are <u>two tricky things</u> with this one. First there's the 'Δv', which means working out the '<u>change in speed</u>', as shown in the example below, rather than just putting a <u>simple value</u> for speed in.
Secondly there's the <u>units</u> of acceleration, which are m/s^2.
<u>Not m/s</u>, which is <u>speed</u>, but m/s^2. Got it? No? Let's try once more: <u>Not m/s</u>, but m/s^2.

    <u>EXAMPLE:</u> A skulking cat accelerates from **2 m/s** to **6 m/s** in **5.6 s**. Find its acceleration.
    <u>ANSWER:</u> Using the formula triangle: $a = \Delta v/t = (6 - 2) / 5.6 = 4 \div 5.6 = \underline{0.71 \ m/s^2}$

Speed-Time Graphs

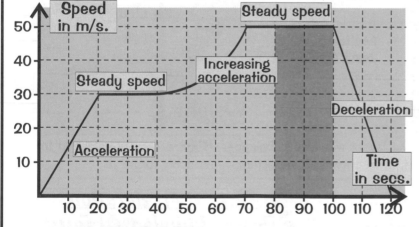

Very Important Notes:

1) <u>GRADIENT = ACCELERATION</u>.
2) <u>Flat sections</u> represent <u>steady speed</u>.
3) The <u>steeper</u> the graph, the <u>greater</u> the <u>acceleration</u> or deceleration.
4) <u>Uphill</u> sections (/) are <u>acceleration</u>.
5) <u>Downhill</u> sections (\) — <u>deceleration</u>.
6) The <u>area</u> under any section of the graph (or all of it) is equal to the <u>distance travelled</u> in that <u>time interval</u>.
7) A <u>curve</u> means <u>changing acceleration</u>.

Calculating Acceleration, Speed and Distance from a Speed-Time Graph

1) The <u>acceleration</u> represented by the <u>first section</u> of the graph is:

    $\text{Acceleration} = \text{gradient} = \dfrac{\text{vertical}}{\text{horizontal}} = \dfrac{30}{20} = \underline{1.5 \ m/s^2}$

2) The <u>speed</u> at any point is simply found by <u>reading the value</u> off the <u>speed axis</u>.

3) The <u>distance travelled</u> in any time interval is equal to the <u>area</u>. For example, the distance travelled between t = 80 and t = 100 is equal to the <u>shaded area</u> which is equal to <u>1000 m</u>.

Speed-time graphs — more fun than gravel (just)...

The tricky thing about these two types of graph is that they can look pretty much the same but represent <u>totally different</u> kinds of motion. Make sure you learn the <u>difference</u> between speed and acceleration and know how to calculate both of them. They're easy marks in the exam.

Forces

A <u>force</u> is simply a <u>push</u> or a <u>pull</u>. There are only <u>six different forces</u> for you to know about:

1) <u>GRAVITY</u> or <u>WEIGHT</u> always acting <u>straight downwards</u>.
   (On Earth, gravity makes all things <u>accelerate towards the ground</u> at about <u>10 m/s²</u>.)
2) <u>REACTION FORCE</u> from a <u>surface</u>, usually acting <u>straight upwards</u>.
3) <u>THRUST</u> or <u>PUSH</u> or <u>PULL</u> due to an engine or rocket <u>speeding something up</u>.
4) <u>DRAG</u> or <u>AIR RESISTANCE</u> or <u>FRICTION</u> which is <u>slowing the thing down</u>.
5) <u>LIFT</u> due to an <u>aeroplane wing</u>.
6) <u>TENSION</u> in a <u>rope</u> or <u>cable</u>.

And there are basically only <u>five different force diagrams</u>:

1) *Stationary Object — All Forces in Balance*

1) The force of <u>GRAVITY</u> (or weight) is acting <u>downwards</u>.
2) This causes a <u>REACTION FORCE</u> from the surface <u>pushing up</u> on the object.
3) This is the <u>only way</u> it can be in <u>BALANCE</u>.
4) <u>Without</u> a reaction force, it would <u>accelerate downwards</u> due to the pull of gravity.
5) The two <u>HORIZONTAL</u> forces must be <u>equal and opposite</u> otherwise the object will <u>accelerate sideways</u>.

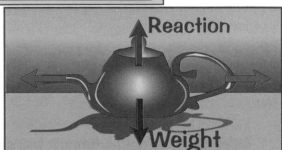

2) *Steady Horizontal Speed — All Forces in Balance!*

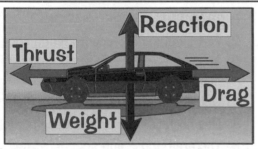

3) *Steady Vertical Speed — All Forces in Balance!*

This skydiver is free-falling at '<u>terminal speed</u>' — see next page.

<u>Take note</u> — to move with a <u>steady speed</u> the forces must be in <u>balance</u>. If there is an <u>unbalanced force</u> then you get <u>acceleration</u>, not steady speed. That's <u>rrrreally important</u> — so don't forget it.

4) *Horizontal Acceleration — Unbalanced Forces*

1) You only get <u>acceleration</u> with an overall <u>resultant</u> (unbalanced) <u>force</u>.
2) The <u>bigger</u> this <u>unbalanced force</u>, the <u>greater</u> the <u>acceleration</u>.

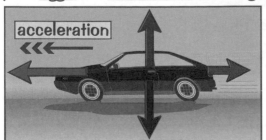

Note that the forces in the <u>other direction</u> (up and down) are still <u>balanced</u>.

5) *Vertical Acceleration — Unbalanced Forces*

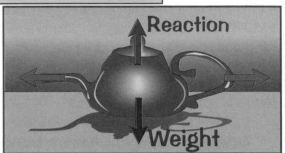

Just after dropping out of the plane, the skydiver accelerates — see next page.

Accelerate your learning — force yourself to revise...

So, things <u>only accelerate</u> in a particular direction if there's an <u>overall force</u> in that direction. Simple.

Friction Forces and Terminal Speed

Friction is Always There to Slow things Down

1) If an object has <u>no force</u> propelling it along, it will always <u>slow down and stop</u> because of <u>friction</u> (unless you're out in space where there's no friction).
2) To travel at a <u>steady speed</u>, things always need a <u>driving force</u> to <u>counteract</u> the friction.
3) Friction occurs in <u>three main ways</u>:

a) **FRICTION BETWEEN SOLID SURFACES WHICH ARE GRIPPING** (static friction)

b) **FRICTION BETWEEN SOLID SURFACES WHICH ARE SLIDING PAST EACH OTHER**

You can <u>reduce</u> both these types of friction by putting a <u>lubricant</u> like <u>oil</u> or <u>grease</u> between the surfaces.

c) **RESISTANCE OR "DRAG" FROM FLUIDS (LIQUIDS OR GASES, e.g. AIR)**

The most important factor <u>by far</u> in <u>reducing drag in fluids</u> is keeping the shape of the object <u>streamlined</u>, like sports cars or boat hulls. Lorries and caravans have "<u>deflectors</u>" on them to make them more streamlined and reduce drag. <u>Roof boxes</u> on cars spoil this shape and so slow them down.
For a given thrust, the <u>higher</u> the <u>drag</u> the <u>lower</u> the <u>top speed</u> of the car.
The <u>opposite extreme</u> to a sports car is a <u>parachute</u> which is about as <u>high drag</u> as you can get — which is, of course, <u>the whole idea</u>.

In a <u>fluid</u>: **FRICTION ALWAYS INCREASES AS THE SPEED INCREASES** — and don't you forget it.

Free-Fallers Reach a Terminal Speed

When free-falling objects <u>first set off</u> they have <u>much more</u> force <u>accelerating</u> them than <u>resistance</u> slowing them down. As the <u>speed</u> increases the resistance <u>builds up</u>. This gradually <u>reduces</u> the <u>acceleration</u> until eventually the <u>resistance force</u> is <u>equal</u> to the <u>accelerating force</u> and then it won't be able to accelerate any more. It will have reached its maximum speed or <u>terminal speed</u>.

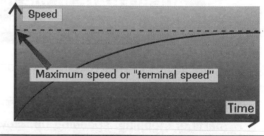

The Terminal Speed of Falling Objects Depends on Their Shape and Area

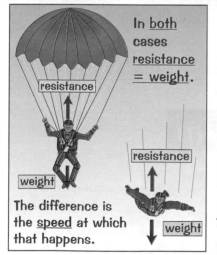

In <u>both</u> cases resistance = weight. The difference is the <u>speed</u> at which that happens.

The <u>accelerating force</u> acting on <u>all falling objects</u> is gravity and it would make them all accelerate at the <u>same rate</u>, if it wasn't for <u>air resistance</u>.
To prove this, on the Moon, where there's <u>no air</u>, hamsters and feathers dropped simultaneously will <u>hit the ground together</u>. However, on Earth, air resistance causes things to fall at <u>different speeds</u>, and the <u>terminal speed</u> of any object is determined by its <u>drag</u> compared to its <u>weight</u>. The drag depends on its <u>shape and area</u>.
The most important example is the <u>human skydiver</u>. Without his parachute open he has quite a <u>small area</u> and a force equal to his <u>weight</u> pulling him down. He reaches a <u>terminal speed</u> of about <u>120 mph</u>. But with the parachute <u>open</u>, there's much more <u>air resistance</u> (at any given speed) and still only the same force pulling him down. This means his <u>terminal speed</u> comes right down to about <u>15 mph</u>, which is a <u>safe speed</u> to hit the ground at.

Air resistance — it can be a real drag...

As well as stopping parachutists ending up as nasty messes on the floor, friction's good for <u>other stuff</u> too. Without friction, you wouldn't be able to walk or run or skip or write... hmm, not all bad then.

Forces and Acceleration

Things only accelerate or change direction if you give them a push. Makes sense.

A Balanced Force Means Steady Speed and Direction

> If the forces on an object are all <u>BALANCED</u>, then it'll keep moving at the <u>SAME SPEED</u> in the <u>SAME DIRECTION</u> (so if it starts off still, it'll stay still).

1) When a train or car or bus or anything else is <u>moving</u> at a <u>constant speed</u>, without changing <u>direction</u>, then the <u>forces</u> on it must all be <u>balanced</u>.

2) Never let yourself entertain the <u>ridiculous idea</u> that things need a constant overall force to <u>keep</u> them moving — NO NO NO NO NO NO!

3) To keep going at a <u>steady speed</u>, there must be <u>zero resultant (overall) force</u> — and don't you forget it.

A Resultant Force Means Acceleration

> If there is an <u>UNBALANCED FORCE</u>, then the object will <u>ACCELERATE</u> in the direction of the force. The size of the acceleration is decided by the formula: F = ma (see below).

1) An <u>unbalanced force</u> will always produce <u>acceleration</u> (or deceleration).

2) This '<u>acceleration</u>' can take <u>five</u> different forms: <u>starting</u>, <u>stopping</u>, <u>speeding up</u>, <u>slowing down</u> and <u>changing direction</u>.

3) On a <u>force diagram</u>, the <u>arrows</u> will be <u>unequal</u>:

The Overall Unbalanced Force is Often Called the Resultant Force

Any <u>resultant force</u> will produce <u>acceleration</u> and this is the <u>formula</u> for it:

$$F = ma \quad \text{or} \quad a = F/m$$

m = mass, a = acceleration, F is always the <u>resultant force</u>

Three Points Which Should be Obvious:

1) The bigger the <u>force</u>, the <u>greater</u> the <u>acceleration</u> or <u>deceleration</u>.

2) The bigger the <u>mass</u>, the <u>smaller the acceleration</u>.

3) To get a <u>big mass</u> to accelerate <u>as fast</u> as a <u>small mass</u>, it needs a <u>bigger force</u>. Just think about pushing <u>heavy trolleys</u> and it should all seem <u>fairly obvious</u>, I would hope.

Module P3 — Forces for Transport

Forces and Acceleration

Resultant Force is Real Important — Especially for "F = ma"

The notion of <u>resultant force</u> is a really important one for you to get your head round.
It's not especially tricky, it's just that it seems to get kind of <u>ignored</u>.
In most <u>real</u> situations there are at least <u>two forces</u> acting on an object along any direction.
The <u>overall</u> effect of these forces will decide the <u>motion</u> of the object — whether it will <u>accelerate</u>,
<u>decelerate</u> or stay at a <u>steady speed</u>. If the forces all point along the same direction, the "<u>overall effect</u>"
is found by just <u>adding or subtracting</u> them. The overall force you get is called the <u>resultant force</u>.
And when you use the <u>formula</u> "<u>F = ma</u>", F must always be the <u>resultant force</u>.

<u>Example</u>: A car of mass of 1750 kg has an engine which provides a driving force of 5200 N.
At 70 mph the drag force acting on the car is 5150 N.
Find its acceleration a) when first setting off from rest b) at 70 mph.
<u>ANSWER</u>: 1) First draw a force diagram for both cases (no need to show the vertical forces):

2) Work out the resultant force in each case, and apply "F = ma" using the formula triangle:

Resultant force = 5200 N
a = F/m = 5200 ÷ 1750 = <u>3.0 m/s²</u>

Resultant force = 5200 − 5150 = 50 N
a = F/m = 50 ÷ 1750 = <u>0.03 m/s²</u>

Reaction Forces

**If object A <u>EXERTS A FORCE</u> on object B then object B
exerts <u>THE EXACT OPPOSITE FORCE</u> on object A.**

1) That means if you <u>push</u> something, say a shopping trolley, the trolley will <u>push back</u> against you,
<u>just as hard</u>.

2) And as soon as you <u>stop</u> pushing, <u>so does the trolley</u>. Kinda clever really.

3) So far so good. The slightly tricky thing to get your head round is this — if the forces are always
equal, <u>how does anything ever go anywhere</u>? The important thing to remember is that the two forces
are acting on <u>different objects</u>. Think about a pair of ice skaters:

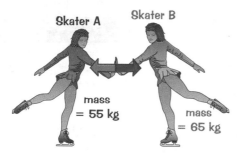

When skater A pushes on skater B (the '<u>action</u>' force),
she feels an equal and opposite force from skater B's
hand (the '<u>reaction</u>' force). Both skaters feel the <u>same
sized force</u>, in <u>opposite directions</u>, and so accelerate
away from each other.

Skater A will be <u>accelerated</u> more than skater B, though,
because she has a smaller mass — remember <u>F = ma</u>.

4) It's the same sort of thing when you go <u>swimming</u>. You <u>push</u> back against the <u>water</u> with your arms
and legs, and the water pushes you forwards with an <u>equal-sized force</u> in the <u>opposite direction</u>.

I have a reaction to forces — they bring me out in a rash...

This is the real deal. Like... proper Physics. It was <u>pretty fantastic</u> at the time — suddenly people
understood how forces and motion worked, they could work out the <u>orbits of planets</u> and everything.
Inspired? No? Shame. Learn them anyway — you're really going to struggle in the exam if you don't.

Stopping Distances

The stopping distance of a car is the distance covered in the time between the driver <u>first spotting</u> a hazard and the car coming to a <u>complete stop</u>. They're pretty keen on this for exam questions, so make sure you <u>learn it properly</u>.

Many Factors Affect Your Total Stopping Distance

The distance it takes to stop a car is divided into the <u>**THINKING DISTANCE**</u> and the <u>**BRAKING DISTANCE**</u>.

1) Thinking Distance

"<u>The distance the car travels in the split-second between a hazard appearing and the driver applying the brakes.</u>"

It's affected by <u>THREE MAIN FACTORS</u>:

a) <u>How FAST you're going</u> — obviously. Whatever your reaction time, the <u>faster</u> you're going, the <u>further</u> you'll go.

b) <u>How DOPEY you are</u> — This is affected by <u>tiredness</u>, <u>drugs</u>, <u>alcohol</u>, <u>old age</u>, and a <u>careless</u> blasé attitude.

c) <u>How hard you're CONCENTRATING</u> — If you're <u>distracted</u> or you're just <u>not concentrating</u>, it'll take longer for you to spot hazards.

The figures below for typical stopping distances are from the Highway Code. It's frightening to see just how far it takes to stop when you're going at 70 mph.

2) Braking Distance

"<u>The distance the car travels during its deceleration whilst the brakes are being applied.</u>"

It's affected by <u>FOUR MAIN FACTORS</u>:

a) <u>How FAST you're going</u> — The <u>faster</u> you're going the <u>further</u> it takes to stop. More details on page 44.

b) <u>How HEAVILY LOADED the vehicle is</u> — With the <u>same</u> brakes, a <u>heavily laden</u> vehicle takes <u>longer to stop</u>. A car won't stop as quickly when it's full of people and luggage and towing a caravan.

c) <u>How good your BRAKES are</u> — All brakes must be checked and maintained <u>regularly</u>. Worn or faulty brakes will let you down <u>catastrophically</u> just when you need them the <u>most</u>, i.e. in an <u>emergency</u>.

d) <u>How good the GRIP is</u> — This depends on <u>THREE THINGS</u>:
1) <u>road surface</u>, 2) <u>weather</u> conditions, 3) <u>tyres</u>.

30 mph	50 mph	70 mph
9m	15m	21m
14m	38m	75m
6 car lengths	13 car lengths	24 car lengths

Thinking distance

Braking distance

So even at <u>30 mph</u>, you should drive no closer than <u>6 or 7 car lengths</u> away from the car in front — just in case. This is why <u>speed limits</u> are so important, and some <u>residential areas</u> are now <u>20 mph zones</u>.

Leaves and diesel spills and muck on t'road are <u>serious hazards</u> because they're <u>unexpected</u>. <u>Wet</u> or <u>icy roads</u> are always much more <u>slippy</u> than dry roads, but often you only discover this when you try to <u>brake</u> hard! Tyres should have a minimum <u>tread depth</u> of <u>1.6 mm</u>. This is essential for getting rid of the <u>water</u> in wet conditions. Without <u>tread</u>, a tyre will simply <u>ride</u> on a <u>layer of water</u> and skid <u>very easily</u>. This is called '<u>aquaplaning</u>' and isn't nearly as cool as it sounds.

Stop right there — and learn this page...

Scary stuff. Makes you think, doesn't it. Learn all the details and write yourself a <u>mini-essay</u> to see how much you really know. You might have to interpret charts of stopping distances in your exam.

Car Safety

When a Car is Moving It Has Kinetic Energy

1) A <u>moving car</u> can have a lot of <u>kinetic energy</u>. To slow a car down this kinetic energy needs to be <u>converted into other types of energy</u> (using the law of conservation of energy).

2) <u>Car brakes</u> slow a car down by turning its kinetic energy into <u>heat energy</u>. This means that when a driver uses the brakes to slow down, the brake pads can become <u>extremely hot</u>.

Cars are Designed to Convert Kinetic Energy Safely in a Crash

1) If a car crashes it will <u>slow down very quickly</u> — this means that a lot of <u>kinetic energy</u> is converted into other forms of energy in a <u>short amount of time</u>, which can be dangerous for the <u>people</u> inside.

2) Cars are <u>designed</u> to convert the <u>kinetic energy</u> of the car and its passengers in a way that is <u>safest</u> for the car's occupants.

3) <u>Crumple zones</u> are parts of the car at the front and back that crumple up in a <u>collision</u>. Some of the car's kinetic energy is converted into other forms of energy by the car body as it <u>changes shape</u>.

4) <u>Seat belts</u> and <u>air bags</u> slow the passengers down <u>safely</u> by converting their kinetic energy into other forms of energy over a longer period of time (see below). These safety features also <u>prevent</u> the passengers from hitting <u>hard surfaces</u> inside the car.

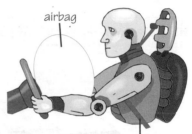

Seat belts absorb energy by stretching the material of the belt. The seat belt won't be as strong after a crash so it has to be replaced.

airbag

seat belt

Safety Features Reduce the Forces Acting in Accidents

Cars have many <u>safety features</u> that are designed to <u>reduce the forces</u> acting on people involved in an accident. Smaller forces mean <u>less severe injuries</u>.

1) In a collision the <u>force</u> on the object can be lowered by <u>slowing the object down</u> over a <u>longer time</u> (you can see this by using the formula $F = ma$ — for the same mass, reducing the deceleration, a, reduces the size of the force, F).

2) <u>Safety features</u> in a car <u>increase the collision time</u> to <u>reduce the forces</u> on the passengers — e.g. crumple zones allow the car to slow down more <u>gradually</u> as parts of it change shape.

3) <u>Roads</u> can also be made safer by placing structures like <u>crash barriers</u> and <u>escape lanes</u> in dangerous locations (like on sharp bends or steep hills). These structures <u>increase the time</u> of any collision — which means the <u>collision force</u> is <u>reduced</u>.

Active Safety Features Take Control in an Emergency

1) Many cars have <u>active safety features</u> — these are features that <u>interact</u> with the way the car drives to help to <u>avoid a crash</u>, e.g. power assisted steering, traction control etc.

2) <u>ABS brakes</u> are an active safety feature that <u>prevent skidding</u>. They help the driver to <u>stay in control</u> of the car when braking sharply. They can also give the car a <u>shorter stopping distance</u>.

Actively learn this — it's the safest way to pass the exam...

The most important thing to learn here is that the <u>forces</u> acting on someone in a crash can be <u>reduced</u> by increasing the <u>collision time</u> — and there are loads of different safety features designed to do this...

Car Safety

Not all safety features help avoid accidents — there are many different ways to make driving safer...

Passive Safety Features Protect People from Injury

1) A <u>passive safety feature</u> is any non-interactive feature of a car that helps to keep the <u>occupants</u> of the car <u>safe</u> — e.g. seat belts, air bags, headrests, etc.

2) A <u>safety cage</u> is a passive safety feature that surrounds the people in a car. This rigid cage <u>protects</u> the passengers because it doesn't easily <u>change shape</u>, even in a severe collision.

3) It's important that the <u>driver</u> of a car is <u>not distracted</u> when driving — and there are many features in a car that have been designed to keep the driver's attention firmly focused <u>on the road</u>.

4) Many cars now have more of their <u>controls</u> either placed on the <u>steering wheel</u> or on <u>control paddles</u> located near the steering wheel. These features allow drivers to stay safely in control of the vehicle while operating the stereo, electric windows, cruise control, etc.

5) Cars are also designed to keep drivers <u>comfortable</u> and in the <u>correct driving position</u> with features like adjustable seats, ventilation, etc.

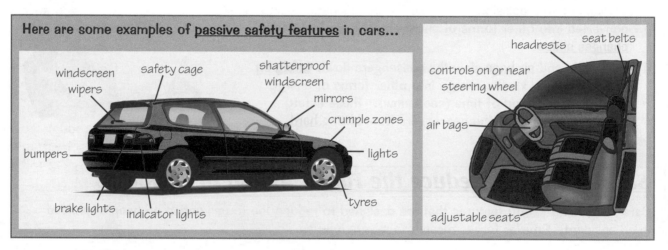

Here are some examples of <u>passive safety features</u> in cars...

windscreen wipers · safety cage · shatterproof windscreen · mirrors · crumple zones · lights · bumpers · brake lights · indicator lights · tyres

headrests · seat belts · controls on or near steering wheel · air bags · adjustable seats

Safety Features Save Lives

1) Safety features are <u>rigorously tested</u> by car manufacturers and government organisations to see how <u>effectively</u> they <u>save lives</u> or <u>prevent injuries</u> in an accident.

2) <u>Crash tests</u> have shown that wearing a <u>seat belt</u> reduces the number of <u>fatalities</u> (deaths) in car accidents by about 50% and that <u>airbags</u> reduce the number of fatalities by about 30% — so they're well worth using.

Road Casualties Great Britain 2004: Annual Report

Graph: Fatalities and serious injuries (thousands) vs Year, showing a downward trend from about 35 thousand in 1980 to about 16 thousand in 2000.

3) The <u>graph</u> (from the Department of Transport) shows the <u>trend</u> in the number of deaths and serious injuries from <u>road traffic accidents</u> in the UK since 1980. It shows that about <u>half as many people</u> are killed or seriously injured nowadays as in 1980 — this <u>reduction</u> is probably due to the wide range of <u>safety features</u> found in cars today.

4) But even though cars are <u>loads safer</u> than they used to be, lots of people still <u>die</u> on the roads every year — often because of <u>bad driving</u> (e.g. <u>speeding</u>, <u>drink-driving</u>, etc.).

Belt up and start revising...

Passengers in the back of cars who don't wear a seat belt will hit the front seat with a force of between <u>30 to 60 times</u> their body's weight in an accident at 30 mph — this is like the force you'd feel if you were sat on by an <u>elephant</u> (which I really wouldn't recommend).

Work and Potential Energy

When a force moves an object, ENERGY IS TRANSFERRED and WORK IS DONE.

That statement sounds far more complicated than it needs to. Try this:

1) Whenever something moves, something else is providing some sort of 'effort' to move it.
2) The thing putting the effort in needs a supply of energy (like fuel or food or electricity, etc.).
3) It then does 'work' by moving the object — and one way or another it transfers the energy it receives (as fuel) into other forms.
4) Whether this energy is transferred 'usefully' (e.g. by lifting a load) or is 'wasted' (e.g. lost as heat through friction), you can still say that 'work is done'. Just like Batman and Bruce Wayne, 'work done' and 'energy transferred' are indeed 'one and the same'. (And they're both given in joules.)

It's Just Another Trivial Formula:

Work Done = Force × Distance

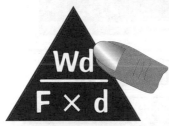

Whether the force is friction or weight or tension in a rope, it's always the same. To find how much energy has been transferred (in joules), you just multiply the force in N by the distance moved in m. Easy as that. I'll show you...

EXAMPLE: Some hooligan kids drag an old tractor tyre 5 m over rough ground. They pull with a total force of 340 N. Find the energy transferred.
ANSWER: Wd = F×d = 340 × 5 = 1700 J. Phew — easy peasy isn't it?

Potential Energy is Energy Due to Height

Potential Energy = mass × g × height

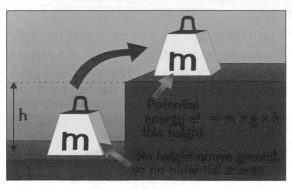

The proper name for this kind of 'potential energy' is gravitational potential energy, (as opposed to 'elastic potential energy' or 'chemical potential energy', etc.). The proper name for g is 'gravitational field strength'. On Earth, g is approximately 10 N/kg.

EXAMPLE: A sheep of mass 47 kg is slowly raised through 6.3 m. Find the gain in potential energy.
ANSWER: Just plug the numbers into the formula:
PE = mgh = 47 × 10 × 6.3 = 2961 J
(Joules because it's energy.)

Revise work done — what else...

Remember "energy transferred" and "work done" are the same thing. If you need a force to make something speed up (P.38), all that means is that you need to give it a bit of energy. Makes sense.

Kinetic Energy

Kinetic Energy is Energy of Movement

Anything that's moving has kinetic energy.
There's a slightly tricky formula for it, so you have to concentrate a little bit harder for this one.
But hey, that's life — it can be real tough sometimes:

$$\text{Kinetic Energy} = \tfrac{1}{2} \times \text{mass} \times \text{speed}^2$$

EXAMPLE: A car of mass 2450 kg is travelling at 38 m/s.
Calculate its kinetic energy.
ANSWER: It's pretty easy. You just plug the numbers into the formula — but watch the 'v²'!
K.E. = ½mv² = ½ × 2450 × 38² = 1 768 900 J (Joules because it's energy.)

Remember, the kinetic energy of something depends both on mass and speed.
The more it weighs and the faster it's going, the bigger its kinetic energy will be.

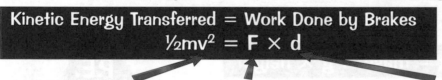

small mass, not fast
low kinetic energy

big fast
lorries Ltd

big mass, real fast
high kinetic energy

Stopping Distances Increase Alarmingly with Extra Speed

— Mainly Because of the v² Bit in K.E.=½mv²

To stop a car, the kinetic energy, ½mv², has to be converted to heat energy at the brakes and tyres:

$$\text{Kinetic Energy Transferred} = \text{Work Done by Brakes}$$
$$\tfrac{1}{2}mv^2 = F \times d$$

v = speed of car   F = maximum braking force   d = braking distance

Learn this real good: if you double the speed, you double the value of v, but the v² means that the K.E. is then increased by a factor of four. However, 'F' is always the maximum possible braking force which can't be increased, so d must also increase by a factor of four to make the equation balance, i.e. if you go twice as fast, the braking distance 'd' must increase by a factor of four to dissipate the extra K.E.

Falling Objects Convert P.E. into K.E.

When something falls, its potential energy is converted into kinetic energy.
So the further it falls, the faster it goes.
In practice, some of the P.E. will be dissipated as heat due to air resistance, but in exam questions they'll likely say you can ignore air resistance, in which case you'll just need to remember this simple and really quite obvious formula:

$$\text{Kinetic energy gained} = \text{Potential Energy lost}$$

Kinetic energy — just get a move on and learn it, OK...

So that's why braking distance goes up so much with speed. Bet you've been dying to find that out — and now you know. What you probably don't know yet, though, is that rather lovely formula at the top of the page. I mean, gosh, it's got more than three letters in it. Get learning.

Gravity and Roller Coasters

Gravity attracts <u>all masses</u>, but you only notice it when one of the masses is <u>really, really big</u> — like a planet. It makes everything accelerate towards the mass. On Earth, it gives things <u>weight</u>.

The Very Important Formula Relating Mass, Weight and Gravity

$$W = m \times g$$

(Weight = mass × g)

1) <u>Mass</u> is the amount of '<u>stuff</u>' in an object. For any given object, this will have the <u>same value anywhere in the Universe</u>. Mass is measured in <u>kg</u>.

2) <u>Weight and mass are NOT the same</u>. Weight is caused by the pull of gravity. It's a <u>force</u> and it's measured in <u>newtons</u> (N).

3) The letter 'g' represents the <u>strength of the gravity</u> and its value is <u>different</u> for <u>different planets</u>. <u>On Earth</u> g is about 10 N/kg. On the <u>Moon</u>, where the gravity is weaker, g is just 1.6 N/kg.

4) This formula is <u>hideously easy</u> to use:

   <u>EXAMPLE</u>: What is the weight, in newtons, of a 5 kg mass, both on Earth and on the Moon?
   <u>ANSWER</u>: W = m × g. On Earth: W = 5 × 10 = <u>50 N</u> (The weight of the 5 kg mass is 50 N)
   On the Moon: W = 5 × 1.6 = <u>8 N</u>   (The weight of the 5 kg mass is 8 N)
   See what I mean. Hideously easy — as long as you've learnt what all the letters mean.

Roller Coasters Transfer Energy

1) At the top of a roller coaster (position A) the carriage has lots of <u>gravitational potential energy</u> (P.E.)

2) As the carriage descends to position B, P.E. is transferred to <u>kinetic energy</u> (K.E.) and the carriage speeds up.

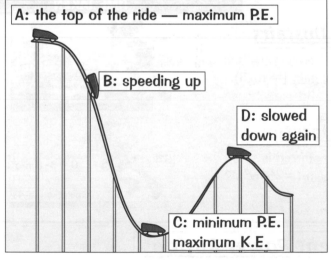

A: the top of the ride — maximum P.E.

B: speeding up

D: slowed down again

C: minimum P.E. maximum K.E.

3) Between positions B and C the carriage keeps <u>accelerating</u> as its P.E. is converted into K.E.

4) If you <u>ignore</u> any <u>air resistance</u> or <u>friction</u> between the carriage and the track, then the carriage will have as much <u>energy</u> at C as it did at A. That energy must have been converted from P.E. to K.E. so at C the carriage has <u>minimum P.E.</u> and <u>maximum K.E.</u>

5) In a real roller coaster (that <u>does</u> have friction to deal with), the carriage has to have enough <u>kinetic energy</u> at point C to carry it up the hill again to D.

Learn about gravity NOW — no point in "weighting" around...

If the formula W = mg seems strangely familiar that's because it's just <u>F = ma in disguise</u> — where 'W' is just the force on an object due to gravity and 'g' is the acceleration of the object caused by gravity.

Power

Power is the 'Rate of Doing Work' — i.e. How Much per Second

POWER is <u>not</u> the same thing as <u>force</u>, nor <u>energy</u>. A <u>powerful</u> machine is not necessarily one which can exert a strong <u>force</u> (though it usually ends up that way).
A <u>POWERFUL</u> machine is one which transfers <u>A LOT OF ENERGY IN A SHORT SPACE OF TIME</u>. This is the <u>very easy formula</u> for power:

$$\text{Power} = \frac{\text{Work done}}{\text{Time taken}}$$

<u>EXAMPLE:</u> A motor transfers 4.8 kJ of useful energy in 2 minutes. Find its power output.
<u>ANSWER:</u> P = Wd / t = 4800/120 = 40 W (or 40 J/s)
(Note that the kJ had to be turned into J, and the minutes into seconds.)

4.8 kJ of useful energy in <u>2 minutes</u>

Power is Measured in Watts (or J/s)

The proper unit of power is the <u>watt</u>. <u>One watt = 1 joule of energy transferred per second</u>.
<u>Power</u> means 'how much energy <u>per second</u>', so <u>watts</u> are the same as '<u>joules per second</u>' (J/s). Don't ever say 'watts per second' — it's <u>nonsense</u>.

Calculating Your Power Output

Both cases use the same formula:

$$\text{POWER} = \frac{\text{ENERGY TRANSFERRED}}{\text{TIME TAKEN}} \quad \text{or} \quad P = \frac{E}{t}$$

a) The Timed Run Upstairs:

In this case the '<u>energy transferred</u>' is simply the <u>potential energy you gain</u> (= mgh).
Hence, <u>power = mgh/t</u>

62kg   12m
Time taken =14s

Power output
= En. transferred/time
= mgh/t
= (62×10×12)÷14
= <u>531 W</u>

b) The Timed Acceleration:

This time the <u>energy transferred</u> is the <u>kinetic energy you gain</u> (= ½mv²).
Hence, <u>power = ½mv²/t</u>

62kg   0 ⟶ 8m/s
time taken = 4s

Power output
= En. transferred/time
= ½mv²/t
= (½×62×8²)÷4
= <u>496 W</u>

Cars Have Different Power Ratings

1) The <u>size</u> and <u>design</u> of car engines determine how <u>powerful</u> they are.

2) The more powerful an engine, the more <u>energy</u> it transfers from its <u>fuel</u> every second, so (usually) the higher the fuel consumption, see next page).

3) E.g. the <u>power output</u> of a typical small car will be around 50 kW and a sports car will be about 100 kW (some are <u>much</u> higher).

Sports car power = 100 kW

Small car power = 50 kW

Watt are you waiting for — revise this stuff now...

The power of a car isn't always measured in watts — sometimes you'll see it in a funny unit called brake horsepower. James Watt defined 1 horsepower as the work done when a horse raises a mass of 550 lb (250 kg) through a height of 1 ft (0.3 m) in 1 second... as you do. I'd stick to watts if I were you.

Fuels for Cars

A lot of us use cars to get us around and about, and lorries transport stuff around the country — but these forms of transport would be pretty useless if they didn't have any fuel to get them moving...

Most Cars Run on Fossil Fuels

1) <u>All vehicles</u> need a <u>fuel</u> to make them move — e.g. most cars and lorries use <u>petrol</u> or <u>diesel</u>.

2) Petrol and diesel are fuels that are <u>made from oil</u>, which is a <u>fossil fuel</u>. The <u>pollution</u> released when these fuels are <u>burnt</u> can cause <u>environmental problems</u> like acid rain and climate change.

3) Fossil fuels are <u>non-renewable</u>, so one day they'll <u>run out</u> — not good news if your car runs on petrol.

4) To get around some of the <u>problems</u> with petrol and diesel fuels, scientists are developing engines that run on <u>alternative types of fuel</u>, such as <u>alcohol</u>, <u>liquid petroleum gas</u> (LPG), <u>hydrogen</u> and '<u>bio-diesel</u>'. They're not perfect, though. <u>LPG</u> still comes from fossil fuels — it just has lower emissions. <u>Hydrogen</u> can be produced by the electrolysis of a very dilute acid, but that takes energy that's likely to come from fossil fuels.

5) A few vehicles use <u>large batteries</u> to power <u>electric motors</u>. These vehicles don't release any <u>pollution</u> when they're driven, but their <u>batteries</u> need to be <u>charged</u> using electricity. This electricity is likely to come from <u>power stations</u> that do pollute.

Fuel Consumption is All About the Amount of Fuel Used...

1) The <u>fuel consumption</u> of a car is usually stated as the <u>distance travelled</u> using a <u>certain amount of fuel</u>. Fuel consumption is often given in <u>miles per gallon</u> (mpg) or <u>litres per 100 km</u> (l/100 km) — e.g. a car with a fuel consumption of 5 l/100 km will travel 100 km on 5 litres of fuel.

2) A car's fuel consumption <u>depends</u> on <u>many different things</u> — e.g. the type and size of the engine, how the car is driven, the shape and weight of the car etc.

3) A car will have a <u>high fuel consumption</u> (i.e. use a lot of fuel) if a <u>large force</u> is needed to move it. Using $F = ma$, you can see that the force needed to move a car depends on the <u>mass</u> of the car and its <u>acceleration</u>.

4) A <u>heavy car</u> will need a greater <u>force</u> to accelerate it by a given amount than a lighter car, so the <u>fuel consumption</u> will be higher for the heavy car.

5) <u>Driving style</u> will also affect the fuel consumption — larger accelerations need a greater force and so use more fuel. <u>Frequent braking and acceleration</u> (e.g. when driving in a town) will <u>increase</u> the fuel consumption.

6) <u>Opening the windows</u> will increase a car's fuel consumption — this is because <u>more energy</u> will be needed to overcome the increase in <u>air resistance</u>.

7) The <u>speed</u> a car's travelling at affects fuel consumption as well. Cars work <u>more efficiently</u> at some speeds than others — the most efficient speed is usually between 40 and 55 mph.

Examples of how car design can improve fuel consumption:

The shape of modern cars reduces air resistance.

Cars are made from lightweight materials.

Engines with better fuel efficiency are constantly being designed.

I bet this page has fuelled your enthusiasm...

You might get asked how to reduce the fuel consumption of a car, so it's important that you remember the different ways that fuel consumption can be affected — e.g. <u>friction</u>, <u>air resistance</u>, <u>weight</u>, etc.

Revision Summary for Module P3

Well done, you've made it to the end of another section. There are loads of bits and bobs about forces, motion and fast cars which you definitely have to learn — and the best way to find out what you know is to get stuck in to these lovely revision questions, which you're going to really enjoy (honest)...

1)* Write down the formula for working out speed. Find the speed of a partly chewed mouse which hobbles 3.2 metres in 35 seconds. Find how far he would go in 25 minutes.

2)* A speed camera is set up in a 30 mph (13.4 m/s) zone. It takes two photographs 0.5 s apart. A car travels 6.3 m between the two photographs. Was the car breaking the speed limit?

3) Sketch a typical distance-time graph and point out all the important parts of it.

4) Explain how to calculate speed from a distance-time graph.

5) What is acceleration? What are its units?

6)* Write down the formula for acceleration. What's the acceleration of a soggy pea flicked from rest to a speed of 14 m/s in 0.4 seconds?

7) Sketch a typical speed-time graph and point out all the important parts of it.

8) Explain how to find speed, distance and acceleration from a speed-time graph.

9) What could you do to reduce the friction between two surfaces?

10) Describe how air resistance is affected by speed.

11) Describe the effect on the top speed of a car of adding a roof box. Explain your answer.

12) What is "terminal speed"? What two main factors affect the terminal speed of a falling object?

13) If an object has zero resultant force on it, can it be moving? Can it be accelerating?

14)* Write down the formula relating resultant force and acceleration. A force of 30 N pushes a trolley of mass 4 kg. What will be its acceleration?

15) Explain what a reaction force is and where it pops up.

16) What are the two different parts of the overall stopping distance of a car?

17) List two factors which affect each of the two parts of the stopping distance.

18) Explain how seat belts, crumple zones and air bags are useful in a crash.

19) List three active safety features and three passive safety features of cars. Describe how each one makes driving safer.

20) What's the connection between "work done" and "energy transferred"?

21)* Write down the formula for work done. A crazy dog drags a big branch 12 m over the next-door neighbour's front lawn, pulling with a force of 535 N. How much work was done?

22)* Write down the formula for potential energy. Calculate the increase in potential energy when a box of mass 12 kg is raised through 4.5 m.

23)* What's the formula for kinetic energy? Find the kinetic energy of a 78 kg sheep moving at 23 m/s.

24) How does the kinetic energy formula explain the effect of speed on the stopping distance of a car?

25)* Calculate the kinetic energy of a 78 kg sheep just as it hits the floor after falling through 20 m.

26) Explain the difference between mass and weight. What's the formula for weight?

27)* At the top of a roller coaster ride a carriage has 150 kJ of gravitational P.E. Ignoring friction, how much K.E. will the carriage have at the bottom (where P.E. = 0)?

28) What's the formula for power? What are the units of power?

29)* An electric motor uses 540 kJ of electrical energy in 4.5 minutes. What is its power consumption?

30)* Calculate the power output of a 78 kg sheep which runs 20 m up a staircase in 16.5 seconds.

31) Describe the relationship between the power rating of a car and its fuel consumption.

32) What are the two main fuels used in cars?

33) Electric vehicles don't give out polluting gases directly, but they still cause pollution. Explain why.

34) Give three factors that affect the fuel consumption of a car.

* Answers on page 100.

Static Electricity

Static electricity is all about charges which are **NOT** free to move. This causes them to build up in one place, and it often ends with a <u>spark</u> or a <u>shock</u> when they do finally move.

1) Build-up of Static is Caused by Friction

1) When two <u>insulating</u> materials are <u>rubbed</u> together, electrons will be <u>scraped off one</u> and <u>dumped</u> on the other.

2) This'll leave a <u>positive</u> static charge on one and a <u>negative</u> static charge on the other.

3) <u>Which way</u> the electrons are transferred <u>depends</u> on the <u>two materials</u> involved.

4) Electrically charged objects <u>attract</u> small neutral objects placed near them.
(Try this: rub a balloon on a woolly pully – then put it near tiddly bits of paper and watch them jump.)

5) The classic examples are <u>polythene</u> and <u>acetate</u> rods being rubbed with a <u>cloth</u> <u>duster</u>, as shown in the diagrams.

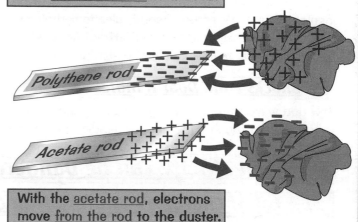

With the <u>polythene rod</u>, electrons move <u>from the duster</u> to the rod.

With the <u>acetate rod</u>, electrons move <u>from the rod</u> to the duster.

2) Only Electrons Move — Never the Positive Charges

<u>Watch out for this in exams</u>. Both +ve and –ve electrostatic charges are only ever produced by the movement of <u>electrons</u>. The positive charges <u>definitely do not move</u>. A positive static charge is always caused by electrons <u>moving</u> away elsewhere, as shown above. Don't forget!

A charged conductor can be <u>discharged safely</u> by connecting it to earth with a <u>metal strap</u>. The electrons flow <u>down</u> the strap to the ground if the charge is <u>negative</u> and flow <u>up</u> the strap from the ground if the charge is <u>positive</u>.

electron flow

electron flow

3) Like Charges Repel, Opposite Charges Attract

Hopefully this is <u>kind of obvious</u>.
Two things with <u>opposite</u> electric charges are <u>attracted</u> to each other.
Two things with the <u>same</u> electric charge will <u>repel</u> each other.
These forces get <u>weaker</u> the <u>further apart</u> the two things are.

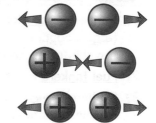

Come on, be +ve — you're half way through the book...

Static electricity's great fun. You must have tried it — rubbing a balloon against your clothes and trying to stick to the ceiling. It really works... well, sometimes. And it's all due to the build-up of hair days are also caused by static — it builds up on your hair, so your strands of hair repel conditioners try to decrease this, but they don't always work...

Static Electricity

They like asking you to give quite detailed examples in exams. Make sure you learn all these details.

Static Electricity Being a Little Joker:

1) Attracting Dust

Dust particles are charged and will be attracted to anything with the opposite charge. Unfortunately, many objects around the house are made out of insulators (e.g. TV screen, wood, plastic containers, etc.) that get easily charged and attract the dust particles — this makes cleaning a nightmare.

2) Clothing Cling and Crackles

When synthetic clothes are dragged over each other (like in a tumble drier) or over your head, electrons get scraped off, leaving static charges on both parts, and that leads to the inevitable — attraction (they stick together and cling to you) and little sparks / shocks as the charges rearrange themselves.

3) Shocks From Door Handles

If you walk on a nylon carpet wearing shoes with insulating soles, charge builds up on your body. Then if you touch a metal door handle, the charge flows to the conductor and you get a little shock.

Static Electricity Can be Dangerous:

1) A Lot of Charge Can Build Up on Clothes

1) A large amount of static charge can build up on clothes made out of synthetic materials if they rub against other synthetic fabrics — like wriggling about on a car seat.

2) Eventually, this charge can become large enough to make a spark — which is really bad news if it happens near any inflammable gases or fuel fumes... KABOOM!

2) Grain Chutes, Paper Rollers and the Fuel Filling Nightmare:

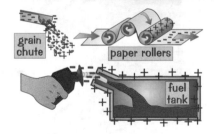

1) As fuel flows out of a filler pipe, or paper drags over rollers, or grain shoots out of pipes, then static can build up.

2) This can easily lead to a spark and might cause an explosion in dusty or fumey places — like when filling up a car with fuel at a petrol station.

3) All these problems with sparks can be solved by earthing charged objects...

Objects Can be Earthed or Insulated to Prevent Sparks

1) Dangerous sparks can be prevented by connecting a charged object to the ground using a conductor (e.g. a copper wire) — this is called earthing and it provides an easy route for the static charges to travel into the ground. This means no charge can build up to give you a shock or make a spark.

2) Fuel tankers must be earthed to prevent any sparks that might cause the fuel to explode.

3) Static charges are also a big problem in places where sparks could ignite inflammable gases, or where there are high concentrations of oxygen (e.g. in a hospital operating theatre).

4) Anti-static sprays and liquids work by making the surface of a charged object conductive — this provides an easy path for the charges to move away and not cause a problem.

Static electricity — it's really shocking stuff...

Lightning always chooses the easiest path between the sky and the ground — even if that
through tall buildings, trees or you. That's why it's never a good idea to fly a kite in a

Uses of Static Electricity

Static electricity isn't always a nuisance. It's got loads of applications in <u>medicine</u> and <u>industry</u>, and now's your chance to learn all about them, you lucky thing...

1) Paint Sprayers — Getting an Even Coat

1) Bikes and cars are painted using <u>electrostatic paint sprayers</u>.

2) The spray gun is <u>charged</u>, which charges up the small drops of paint. Each paint drop <u>repels</u> all the others, since they've all got the <u>same charge</u>, so you get a very <u>fine spray</u>.

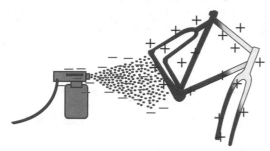

3) The object to be painted is given an <u>opposite charge</u> to the gun. This <u>attracts</u> the fine spray of paint.

4) This method gives an <u>even coat</u> and hardly any paint is <u>wasted</u>. In addition parts of the bicycle or car pointing <u>away</u> from the spray gun <u>still receive paint</u>, i.e. there are no paint <u>shadows</u>.

2) Dust Precipitators — Cleaning Up Emissions

<u>Smoke</u> is made up of <u>tiny particles</u> which can be removed with a precipitator. There are several different designs of precipitator — here's a very simple one:

1) As smoke particles reach the bottom of the chimney, they meet a <u>wire grid</u> with a high <u>negative charge</u>, which charges the particles negatively.

2) The charged smoke particles are <u>attracted</u> to <u>positively</u> charged <u>metal plates</u>. The smoke particles <u>stick together</u> to form larger particles.

3) When <u>heavy enough</u>, the particles <u>fall</u> off the plates or are <u>knocked off</u> by a hammer. The dust falls to the bottom of the chimney and can be removed.

4) The gases coming out of the chimney have <u>very few smoke particles</u> in them.

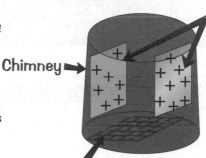

Positively charged collection plates

Chimney →

Negatively charged grid

3) Defibrillators — Restarting a Heart

1) The beating of your heart is controlled by tiny little <u>electrical pulses</u> inside your body. So an <u>electric shock</u> to a <u>stopped heart</u> can make it start beating again.

2) Hospitals and ambulances have machines called <u>defibrillators</u> which can be used to shock a stopped heart back into operation.

3) The defibrillator consists of two <u>paddles</u> connected to a power supply.

4) The paddles of the defibrillator are placed <u>firmly</u> on the patient's chest to get a <u>good electrical contact</u> and then the defibrillator is <u>charged up</u>.

5) Everyone moves away from the patient except for the defibrillator operator who holds <u>insulated handles</u>. This means <u>only the patient</u> gets a shock.

If this doesn't get your heart going — nothing will...

You can get your very <u>own</u> special <u>defibrillator</u> now. One to carry around in your handbag, just in case. really, you can (okay, maybe it wouldn't fit in your handbag unless you're Mary Poppins, but still...). really clever thing is that they don't work unless they're needed. Amazing eh...

Charge in Circuits

If you've got a <u>complete loop</u> (a circuit) of <u>conducting stuff</u> (e.g. metal) connected to an electric power source (like a battery), electricity <u>flows round it</u>. Isn't electricity great.

Mind you it's pretty bad news if the words don't mean anything to you... Hey, I know — learn them now!

1) **CURRENT** is the <u>flow</u> of electrons around the circuit and it's measured in <u>amps</u>, <u>A</u>. Current will <u>only flow</u> through a component if there is a <u>voltage</u> across that component (unless the component is a superconductor).

2) **VOLTAGE** is the <u>driving force</u> that pushes the current round — kind of like "<u>electrical pressure</u>". Voltage is measured in <u>volts</u>, <u>V</u>.

3) **RESISTANCE** is anything in the circuit which <u>slows the flow down</u>. Resistance is measured in <u>ohms</u>, <u>Ω</u>.

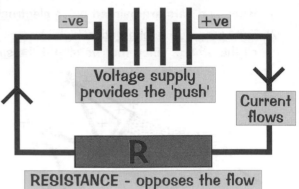

Voltage supply provides the 'push'

Current flows

RESISTANCE - opposes the flow

4) **THERE'S A BALANCE:** the <u>voltage</u> is trying to <u>push</u> the current round the circuit, and the <u>resistance</u> is <u>opposing</u> it — the <u>relative sizes</u> of the voltage and resistance decide <u>how big</u> the current will be:

> If you <u>increase the VOLTAGE</u> — then **MORE CURRENT** will flow.
> If you <u>increase the RESISTANCE</u> — then **LESS CURRENT** will flow
> (or <u>MORE VOLTAGE</u> will be needed to keep the <u>SAME CURRENT</u> flowing).

It's Just Like the Flow of Water Around a Set of Pipes

1) The <u>current</u> is simply like the <u>flow of water</u>.

2) The <u>voltage</u> is like the <u>force</u> provided by a <u>pump</u> which pushes the stuff round.

3) <u>Resistance</u> is any sort of <u>constriction</u> in the flow, which is what the pressure has to <u>work against</u>.

4) If you <u>turn up the pump</u> and provide more <u>force</u> (or "<u>voltage</u>"), the flow will <u>increase</u>.

5) If you put in more <u>constrictions</u> ("<u>resistance</u>"), the flow (current) will <u>decrease</u>.

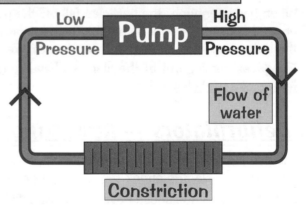

Low Pressure **Pump** High Pressure

Flow of water

Constriction

If You Break the Circuit, the Current Stops Flowing

1) Current only flows in a circuit as long as there's a <u>complete loop</u> for it to flow around. <u>Break</u> the circuit and the <u>current stops</u>.

2) <u>Wire fuses</u> and <u>circuit breakers</u> (resettable fuses) are safety features that break a circuit if there's a fault (see p.53).

Teachers — the driving force of revision...

The funny thing is — the <u>electrons</u> in circuits actually move from <u>–ve to +ve</u>... but scientists always think of <u>current</u> as flowing from <u>+ve to –ve</u>. Basically it's just because that's how the <u>early physicists</u> thought of it (before they found out about the electrons), and now it's become <u>convention</u>.

Module P4 — Radiation for Life

Fuses and Safe Plugs

Now then, did you know... electricity is dangerous. It can kill you. Well just watch out for it, that's all.

Plugs and Cables — Learn the Safety Features

Get the Wiring Right:

1) The <u>right coloured wire</u> is connected to each pin, and <u>firmly screwed</u> in.

2) <u>No bare wires</u> showing inside the plug.

3) <u>Cable grip</u> tightly fastened over the cable <u>outer layer</u>.

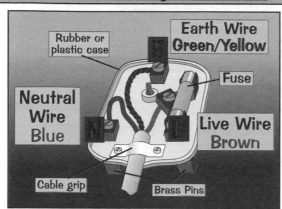

Rubber or plastic case
Earth Wire Green/Yellow
Fuse
Neutral Wire Blue
Live Wire Brown
Cable grip
Brass Pins

Plug Features:

1) The <u>metal parts</u> are made of copper or brass because these are <u>very good conductors</u>.

2) The case, cable grip and cable insulation are made of <u>rubber</u> or <u>plastic</u> because they're really good <u>insulators</u>, and <u>flexible</u> too.

3) This all keeps the electricity flowing <u>where it should</u>.

Earthing and Fuses Prevent Fires and Shocks

The <u>**LIVE WIRE**</u> alternates between a <u>**HIGH +VE AND −VE VOLTAGE**</u> of about <u>230 V</u>.
The <u>**NEUTRAL WIRE**</u> is always at <u>0 V</u>. Electricity normally flows in through the live wire and out through neutral wire.
The <u>**EARTH WIRE**</u> and <u>fuse</u> (or circuit breaker) are just for <u>safety</u> and <u>work together</u> like this:

1) If a <u>fault</u> develops in which the <u>live</u> somehow touches the <u>metal case</u>, then because the case is <u>earthed</u>, a <u>big current</u> flows in through the <u>live</u>, through the <u>case</u> and out down the <u>earth wire</u>.

2) This <u>surge</u> in current <u>'blows' the fuse</u> (or trips the circuit breaker), which <u>cuts off</u> the <u>live supply</u>.

3) This <u>isolates</u> the <u>whole appliance</u>, making it <u>impossible</u> to get an electric <u>shock</u> from the case. It also prevents the risk of <u>fire</u> caused by the heating effect of a large current.

4) <u>Fuses</u> should be <u>rated</u> as near as possible but <u>just higher</u> than the <u>normal operating current</u>.

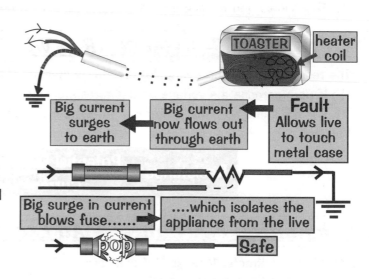

TOASTER
heater coil
Big current surges to earth
Big current now flows out through earth
Fault Allows live to touch metal case
Big surge in current blows fuse......
....which isolates the appliance from the live
POP
Safe

All appliances with <u>metal cases</u> must be "<u>earthed</u>" to reduce the danger of <u>electric shock</u>. "Earthing" just means the case must be attached to an <u>earth wire</u>. An earthed conductor can <u>never become live</u>. If the appliance has a <u>plastic casing</u> and no metal parts <u>showing</u> then it's said to be <u>double insulated</u>. Anything with <u>double insulation</u> like that <u>doesn't need an earth wire</u> — just a live and neutral.

CGP books are ACE — well, I had to get a plug in somewhere...

Have you ever noticed how if anything doesn't work in the house, it's always due to the fuse.
The lights, the toaster, the car — always a little annoying, but it makes everything a <u>whole load safer</u>...

Resistance

A <u>resistor</u> is a component that reduces the current flowing in a circuit. The higher the <u>resistance</u>, the harder it is for the electricity to flow, and so the lower the <u>current</u>.

If you get an electric shock, it's the current that does the damage, not the voltage. So the higher the resistance in a circuit, the smaller the risk of injury.

Variable Resistors

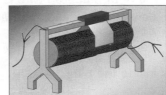

1) A <u>variable resistor</u> is a resistor whose resistance can be <u>changed</u> by twiddling a knob or something.

2) The old-fashioned ones are <u>huge coils of wire</u> with a <u>slider</u> on them.

3) They're great for <u>altering the current</u> flowing through a circuit. Turn the resistance <u>up</u>, the current <u>drops</u>. Turn the resistance <u>down</u>, the current goes <u>up</u>. You can use this to make the <u>standard test circuit</u>:

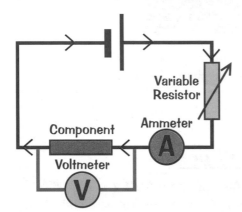

Variable Resistor

Ammeter

Component

Voltmeter

The Ammeter

1) Measures the <u>current</u> (in <u>amps</u>) through the component.
2) Can be put <u>anywhere in series</u> in the <u>main circuit</u>, but never <u>in parallel</u> like the voltmeter.

The Voltmeter

1) Measures the <u>voltage</u> (in <u>volts</u>) across the component.
2) Must be placed <u>in parallel</u> around the <u>component under test</u> — <u>NOT</u> around the variable resistor or the battery!
3) The proper name for voltage is "<u>potential difference</u>".

1) This <u>very basic circuit</u> is used for <u>testing the resistance of components</u>.

2) As you <u>vary</u> the <u>variable resistor</u> it alters the <u>current</u> flowing through the circuit.

3) This allows you to take several <u>pairs of readings</u> from the <u>ammeter</u> and <u>voltmeter</u>.

Calculating Resistance: R = V/I

The resistance of a (non-variable) resistor is <u>steady</u> (at constant temperature).

1) If you <u>increase</u> the <u>voltage</u> across a resistor, the <u>current increases</u> as well.

2) For the same potential difference (p.d.), <u>current increases</u> as <u>resistance decreases</u>.

You can calculate the resistance of a resistor using the formula:

$$\text{Resistance} = \frac{\text{Potential Difference}}{\text{Current}}$$

Calculating Resistance — An Example

EXAMPLE. Voltmeter V reads 6 V and resistor R is 4 Ω. What is the current through ammeter A?

ANSWER. Rearrange the resistance formula to give:
        I = V/R.
Then put in the values: I = 6/4 which is 1.5 A.

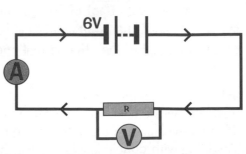

You have to learn this — resistance is futile...

Sometimes you can get funny light switches which <u>fade</u> the light in and out. Some of them work by resistance, and are perfect for getting that nice romantic atmosphere you want for your dinner for two. <u>Learn the equation</u> — you won't be given it in your exam, so you'll lose easy marks if you don't.

Ultrasound Scans and Treatment

Sound is a Longitudinal Wave

You need to know the features of longitudinal waves:

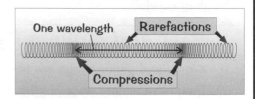

1) Sound waves squash up and stretch out the material they pass through, making compressions and rarefactions.

2) The WAVELENGTH is a full cycle of the wave, e.g. from crest to crest, not just from "two bits that are sort of separated a bit".

3) FREQUENCY is how many complete waves there are per second (passing a certain point). Frequency is measured in hertz. 1 Hz is 1 complete wave per second. For sound, high frequency = high pitch.

4) The AMPLITUDE tells you how much energy the wave is carrying, or how loud the sound is. You can see the amplitude of a sound on a CRO (oscilloscope). CRO displays show sounds as transverse waves so you can see what's going on. You measure the amplitude from the middle line to the crest, NOT from a trough to a crest.

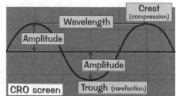

In LONGITUDINAL waves the vibrations are along the SAME DIRECTION as the wave is travelling.	In TRANSVERSE waves the vibrations are at 90° to the DIRECTION OF TRAVEL of the wave.

Ultrasound is Sound with a Higher Frequency Than We Can Hear

Electrical devices can be made which produce electrical oscillations of any frequency. These can easily be converted into mechanical vibrations to produce sound waves beyond the range of human hearing (i.e. frequencies above 20 kHz). This is called ultrasound and it has loads of uses in hospitals:

1) Breaking Down Kidney Stones

An ultrasound beam concentrates high energy waves at the kidney stone and turns it into sand-like particles. These particles then pass out of the body in urine. It's a good method because the patient doesn't need surgery and it's relatively painless.

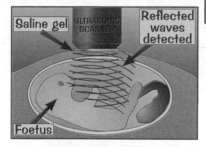

2) For Pre-Natal Scanning of a Foetus

Ultrasound waves can pass through the body, but whenever they reach a boundary between two different media (like fluid in the womb and the skin of the foetus) some of the wave is reflected back and detected. The exact timing and distribution of these echoes are processed by a computer to produce a video image of the foetus.
No one knows for sure whether ultrasound is safe in all cases but X-rays would definitely be dangerous to the foetus.

3) Measuring the Speed of Blood Flow — You don't need to know how they do that though.

Ultrasound Has Advantages over X-Rays

1) X-rays pass easily through soft tissues like muscle and skin, so you can usually only use them to make images of hard things like bone. Ultrasound is great for imaging soft tissue.
   (It's no good for taking pictures of bones though — well, you win some, you lose some.)

2) The other advantage is that ultrasound is, as far as anyone can tell, safe.
   X-rays are ionising radiation. They can cause cancer if you're exposed to too high a dose.

Looking at things with sound — weird if you ask me...

You can use ultrasound to get images of other things too — like shipwrecks. The time it takes for the wave to return also tells you the distance to the object. Dolphins use ultrasound as well (I always knew they were going to take over the world) to detect predators and food. Clever eh...

Module P4 — Radiation for Life

Ionising Radiation

Ionising radiation (e.g. alpha, beta, gamma and X-rays) damages living cells, but can be really useful if handled carefully...

X-Rays and Gamma Rays are Electromagnetic Waves

1) X-rays and gamma rays are both high frequency, short wavelength electromagnetic waves.
2) They have similar wavelengths, and so have similar properties, but are made in different ways:
   a) Gamma rays are released from some unstable atomic nuclei when they decay (see p.57). Nuclear decay is completely random, so there's no way to control when they're released.
   b) X-rays can be produced by firing high-speed electrons at a heavy metal like tungsten. These are much easier to control than gamma rays.

X-Rays are Used in Hospitals, but are Pretty Dangerous

1) Radiographers in hospitals take X-ray photographs of people to see whether they have any broken bones.
2) X-rays pass easily through flesh, but not so easily through denser material like bones or metal.
3) X-rays can cause cancer, so radiographers wear lead aprons and stand behind a lead screen, or leave the room, to keep their exposure to X-rays to a minimum.

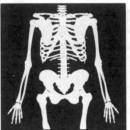

The brighter bits are where fewer X-rays get through. This is a negative image. The plate starts off all white.

Radiation Harms Living Cells

1) Nuclear radiation (alpha α, beta β, gamma γ) and X-rays will cheerfully enter living cells and collide with molecules.
2) These collisions cause ionisation, which damages or destroys the molecules.
3) Lower doses tend to cause minor damage without killing the cell. This can give rise to mutant cells which divide uncontrollably. This is cancer.
4) Higher doses tend to kill cells completely, which causes radiation sickness if a lot of body cells all get blatted at once.

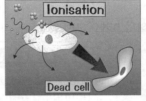

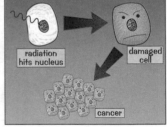

Outside the Body, β and γ Sources are the Most Dangerous

This is because beta and gamma can get inside to the delicate organs, whereas alpha is much less dangerous because it can't penetrate the skin.

Inside The Body, an α Source is the Most Dangerous

Inside the body alpha sources do all their damage in a very localised area. Beta and gamma sources on the other hand are less dangerous inside the body because they are less ionising, and mostly pass straight out without doing much damage.

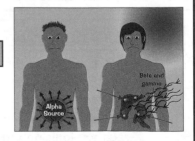

Radiation — easy as α, β, γ...

X-rays aren't just used for looking for broken bones — they have some other uses, such as working out the exact place, size and orientation of a cancer tumour. Several X-rays are needed though, so it's left to a last resort — you don't want to risk causing more damage to the person...

Radioactive Decay

Radioactive materials are made up of atoms that decay, giving out <u>alpha</u>, <u>beta</u> or <u>gamma</u> radiation.

You Need to Know What the Three Types of Radiation Are

<u>ALPHA PARTICLES ARE HELIUM NUCLEI:</u> $^4_2$He
  They're relatively <u>big</u>, <u>heavy</u> and <u>slow moving</u>, so they <u>don't penetrate</u> very far into materials.

<u>BETA PARTICLES ARE FAST-MOVING ELECTRONS:</u> $^0_{-1}$e
  They're <u>quite fast</u> and <u>quite small</u>.

<u>GAMMA RAYS ARE ELECTROMAGNETIC RADIATION:</u> $^0_0\gamma$
  They don't have any <u>mass or charge</u>, so they penetrate a <u>long way</u> before they're stopped.

Radioactivity is a Totally Random Process

<u>Unstable nuclei</u> will <u>decay</u>, and in the process <u>give out radiation</u>. This happens entirely at <u>random</u>. This means that if you have 1000 unstable nuclei, you can't say when <u>any one of them</u> is going to decay, and neither can you do anything at all <u>to make a decay happen</u>.
Each nucleus will just decay quite <u>spontaneously</u> in its <u>own good time</u>. It's completely unaffected by <u>physical</u> conditions like <u>temperature</u>, or by any sort of <u>chemical bonding</u> etc.

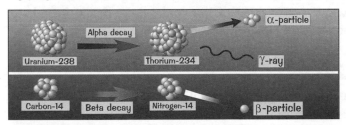

When the nucleus <u>does</u> decay it will <u>spit out</u> one or more of the three types of radiation, <u>alpha</u>, <u>beta</u> and <u>gamma</u>, and in the process the <u>nucleus</u> will often <u>change</u> into a <u>new element</u>.

Nuclear Equations — Not Half as Bad as They Sound

Nuclear equations are OK I think. In the end it's just a case of making sure the <u>mass numbers</u> and <u>atomic numbers balance up on both sides</u>, that's all. The trickiest bit is <u>remembering</u> the <u>mass and atomic numbers</u> for α, β and γ particles, and <u>neutrons</u> too. Make sure you can do all of these <u>easily</u>:

1) Alpha emission:
An α-particle has a mass of 4 and charge of +2: $^4_2$He

A typical <u>alpha emission</u>: $^{226}_{88}$Ra $\rightarrow$ $^{222}_{86}$Rn $+ {^4_2}$He

2) Beta emission:
A β-particle has (virtually) no mass and a charge of –1: $^0_{-1}$e

A typical <u>beta emission</u>: $^{14}_6$C $\rightarrow$ $^{14}_7$N $+ {^0_{-1}}$e

3) Gamma emission:
A γ-ray is a <u>photon</u> with no mass and no charge: $^0_0\gamma$

After an <u>alpha or beta emission</u> the nucleus sometimes has <u>extra energy to get rid of</u>. It does this by emitting a <u>gamma ray</u>. Gamma emission <u>never changes</u> the <u>atomic or mass numbers</u> of the nucleus.
A typical combined α and γ emission: $^{238}_{92}$U $\rightarrow$ $^{234}_{90}$Th $+ {^4_2}$He $+ {^0_0}\gamma$

Sorry, no clear equations on this page...

The most important thing to remember is the symbol for each type of particle with its <u>proton number</u> and <u>mass number</u>. As long as you know those, you should be able to write down an equation for any type of radioactive decay they might throw at you in the exam — just keep everything balanced...

Radioactivity and Half-Life

The <u>unit</u> for measuring <u>radioactivity</u> is the <u>becquerel</u> (Bq). 1 Bq means <u>one nucleus decaying per second</u>.

The Radioactivity of a Sample Always Decreases Over Time

1) This is <u>pretty obvious</u> when you think about it. Each time a <u>decay</u> happens and an alpha, beta or gamma is given out, it means one more <u>radioactive nucleus</u> has <u>disappeared</u>.

2) Obviously, as the <u>unstable nuclei</u> all steadily disappear, the <u>activity as a whole</u> will <u>decrease</u>. So the <u>older</u> a sample becomes, the <u>less radiation</u> it will emit.

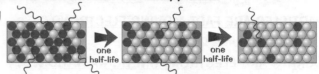

3) <u>How quickly</u> the activity <u>drops off</u> varies a lot. For <u>some</u> substances it takes <u>just a few hours</u> before nearly all the unstable nuclei have <u>decayed</u>, whilst for others it can take <u>millions of years</u>.

4) The problem with trying to <u>measure</u> this is that <u>the activity never reaches zero</u>, which is why we have to use the idea of <u>half-life</u> to measure how quickly the activity <u>drops off</u>.

5) Learn this <u>definition</u> of <u>half-life</u>:

6) A <u>short half-life</u> means the activity falls quickly, because <u>lots</u> of the nuclei decay <u>quickly</u>.

> **HALF-LIFE** is the **TIME TAKEN** for **HALF** of the radioactive atoms now present to **DECAY**

7) A <u>long half-life</u> means the activity <u>falls more slowly</u> because <u>most</u> of the nuclei don't decay <u>for a long time</u> — they just sit there, <u>basically unstable</u>, but kind of <u>biding their time</u>.

Do Half-life Questions Step by Step

Half-life is maybe a little confusing, but exam calculations are <u>straightforward</u> so long as you do them slowly, **STEP BY STEP**. Like this one:

<u>A VERY SIMPLE EXAMPLE:</u> The activity of a radioisotope is 640 cpm (counts per minute). Two hours later it has fallen to 40 cpm. Find the half-life of the sample.

<u>ANSWER:</u> You must go through it in <u>short simple steps</u> like this:

<u>INITIAL</u> <u>count:</u>		after ONE <u>half-life:</u>		after TWO <u>half-lives:</u>		after THREE <u>half-lives:</u>		after FOUR <u>half-lives:</u>
640	$(\div 2) \rightarrow$	320	$(\div 2) \rightarrow$	160	$(\div 2) \rightarrow$	80	$(\div 2) \rightarrow$	40

Notice the careful <u>step-by-step method</u>, which tells us it takes <u>four half-lives</u> for the activity to fall from 640 to 40. Hence <u>two hours</u> represents four half-lives, so the <u>half-life is 30 minutes</u>.

Finding the Half-life of a Sample Using a Graph

1) The data for the graph will usually be <u>several readings</u> of <u>count rate</u> taken with a <u>G-M tube and counter</u>.

2) The <u>graph</u> will always be shaped like the one shown.

3) The <u>half-life</u> is found from the graph, by finding the <u>time interval</u> on the <u>bottom axis</u> corresponding to a <u>halving</u> of the <u>activity</u> on the <u>vertical axis</u>. Easy peasy really.

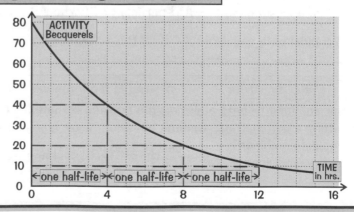

Half-life of a box of chocolates — about five minutes...

For <u>medical applications</u>, you need to use isotopes that have a <u>suitable half-life</u>. A radioactive tracer needs to have a short half-life to minimise the risk of damage to the patient. A source for sterilising equipment needs to have a long half-life, so you don't have to replace it too often (see p.60).

Background Radiation

Background Radiation Comes from Many Sources

The <u>background radiation</u> we receive comes from:

1) Radioactivity of naturally occurring <u>unstable isotopes</u> which are <u>all around us</u> — in the <u>air</u>, in <u>food</u>, in <u>building materials</u> and in the <u>rocks</u> under our feet.

2) Radiation from <u>space</u>, which is known as <u>cosmic rays</u>. These come mostly from the <u>Sun</u>.

3) Radiation due to <u>human activity</u>, e.g. <u>fallout</u> from <u>nuclear explosions</u>, or <u>dumped nuclear waste</u>. But this represents a <u>tiny</u> proportion of the total background radiation.

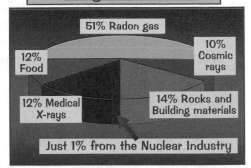

The RELATIVE PROPORTIONS of <u>background radiation</u>:

- 51% Radon gas
- 12% Food
- 10% Cosmic rays
- 12% Medical X-rays
- 14% Rocks and Building materials

Just 1% from the Nuclear Industry

The Level of Background Radiation Changes Depending on Where You Are

1) At <u>high altitudes</u> (e.g. in <u>jet planes</u>) the background radiation <u>increases</u> because of more exposure to <u>cosmic rays</u>. That means commercial pilots have an increased risk of getting some types of cancer.

2) <u>Underground in mines</u>, etc. it increases because of the <u>rocks</u> all around.

3) Certain <u>underground rocks</u> (e.g. granite) can cause higher levels at the <u>surface</u>, especially if they release <u>radioactive radon gas</u>, which tends to get <u>trapped inside people's houses</u>.

Radon Gas is the Subject of Scientific Debate

1) The <u>radon concentration</u> in people's houses <u>varies widely</u> across the UK, depending on what type of <u>rock</u> the house is built on.

2) Studies have shown that exposure to <u>high doses</u> of radon gas can cause <u>lung cancer</u> — and the <u>greater</u> the radon concentration, the <u>higher the risk</u>.

3) The scientific community is a bit divided on the effects of <u>lower doses</u>, and there's still a lot of debate over what the highest safe(ish) concentration is.

4) Evidence suggests that the risk of developing lung cancer from radon is <u>much greater</u> for <u>smokers</u> than non-smokers.

5) Some medical professionals reckon that about <u>1 in 20</u> deaths from <u>lung cancer</u> (about 2000 per year) are caused by radon exposure.

6) <u>New houses</u> in areas where high levels of radon gas might occur must be designed with good <u>ventilation systems</u>. These reduce the concentration of radon in the living space.

7) In <u>existing houses</u>, the Government recommends that ventilation systems are put in wherever the radiation due to radon is above a certain level.

Millom

Coloured bits indicate more radiation from rocks

Background radiation — it's like nasty wallpaper...

Did you know that background radiation was first discovered <u>accidentally</u>. Scientists were trying to work out which materials were radioactive, and couldn't understand why their reader still showed radioactivity when there was <u>no material</u> being tested. They realised it must be natural background radiation.

Medical Uses of Radiation

As well as X-ray scans, ionising radiation has loads of uses in hospitals, and you have to know about them.

1) Radiotherapy — the Treatment of Cancer Using Gamma Rays

1) Since high doses of gamma rays will <u>kill all living cells</u>, they can be used to <u>treat cancers</u>.
2) The gamma rays have to be <u>directed carefully</u> and at just the right <u>dosage</u> so as to kill the <u>cancer cells</u> without damaging too many <u>normal cells</u>.
3) However, a <u>fair bit of damage</u> is <u>inevitably</u> done to <u>normal cells</u>, which makes the patient feel <u>very ill</u>. But if the cancer is <u>successfully killed off</u> in the end, then it's worth it.

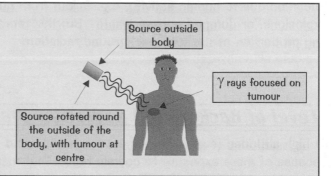

TO TREAT CANCER:
1) The gamma rays are <u>focused</u> on the tumour using a <u>wide beam</u>.
2) This beam is <u>rotated</u> round the patient with the tumour at the centre.
3) This <u>minimises</u> the exposure of <u>normal cells</u> to radiation, and so <u>reduces</u> the chances of damaging the rest of the body.

Source outside body

γ rays focused on tumour

Source rotated round the outside of the body, with tumour at centre

2) Tracers in Medicine — Always Short Half-life Gamma Emitters

1) Certain <u>radioactive isotopes</u> can be <u>injected</u> into people (or they can just <u>swallow</u> them) and their progress <u>around the body</u> can be followed using an external <u>detector</u>. A computer converts the reading to a <u>display</u> showing where the <u>strongest reading</u> is coming from.

2) A well-known example is the use of <u>iodine-131</u>, which is absorbed by the <u>thyroid gland</u> just like normal iodine-127, but it gives out <u>radiation</u> which can be <u>detected</u> to indicate whether or not the thyroid gland is <u>taking in the iodine</u> as it should.

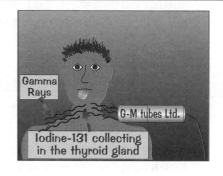

Gamma Rays

G-M tubes Ltd.

Iodine-131 collecting in the thyroid gland

3) <u>All isotopes</u> which are taken <u>into the body</u> must be <u>GAMMA or BETA</u> (never alpha), so that the radiation <u>passes out of the body</u> — and they should only last <u>a few hours</u>, so that the radioactivity inside the patient <u>quickly disappears</u> (i.e. they should have a <u>short half-life</u>).

3) Sterilisation of Surgical Instruments Using Gamma Rays

1) <u>Medical instruments</u> can be <u>sterilised</u> by exposing them to a <u>high dose</u> of <u>gamma rays</u>, which will <u>kill</u> all <u>microbes</u>.
2) The great <u>advantage</u> of <u>irradiation</u> over boiling is that it doesn't involve <u>high temperatures</u>, so heat-sensitive things like <u>thermometers</u> and <u>plastic instruments</u> can be totally <u>sterilised</u> without <u>damaging</u> them.

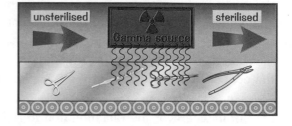

unsterilised   Gamma source   sterilised

Ionising radiation — just what the doctor ordered...

See — radiation isn't all bad. It also kills bad things, like disease-causing bacteria. <u>Radiotherapy</u> and chemotherapy (which uses chemicals instead of gamma rays) are commonly used to treat cancer. They both work in the same way — by killing <u>lots and lots</u> of cells, and trying to <u>target</u> the cancerous ones...

Non-Medical Uses of Radiation

Radioactive materials aren't just used in hospitals (p.60) — you've got to know these uses too.

1) Tracers in Industry — For Finding Leaks

This is much the same technique as the medical tracers.

1) Radioisotopes can be used to <u>track</u> the <u>movement of waste</u> materials, find the <u>route</u> of underground pipe systems or <u>detect leaks or blockages in pipes</u>.

2) To check a pipe, you just <u>squirt it in</u>, then go along the <u>outside</u> with a <u>detector</u>. If the radioactivity <u>reduces</u> or <u>stops</u> after a certain point, there must be a <u>leak</u> or <u>blockage</u> there. This is really useful for <u>concealed</u> or <u>underground</u> pipes, to save you <u>digging up half the road</u> trying to find the leak.

3) The isotope used <u>must</u> be a <u>gamma emitter</u>, so that the radiation can be <u>detected</u> even through <u>metal or earth</u> which may be <u>surrounding</u> the pipe. Alpha and beta radiation wouldn't be much use because they are <u>easily blocked</u> by any surrounding material.

4) It should also have a <u>short half-life</u> so as not to cause a <u>hazard</u> if it collects somewhere.

2) Smoke Detectors

1) A <u>weak</u> radioactive source is placed in the detector, close to <u>two electrodes</u>.
2) The source causes <u>ionisation</u>, and a <u>current</u> flows.
3) If there is a fire then smoke will <u>absorb</u> the radiation — the current falls and the <u>alarm sounds</u>.

3) Radioactive Dating of Rocks and Archaeological Specimens

The discovery of radioactivity and the idea of <u>half-life</u> gave scientists their <u>first opportunity</u> to <u>accurately</u> work out the <u>age</u> of some <u>rocks</u> and <u>archaeological specimens</u>. By measuring the <u>amount</u> of a <u>radioactive isotope</u> left in a sample, and knowing its <u>half-life</u>, you can work out <u>how long</u> the thing has been around.

Radiocarbon Dating — Carbon-14 Calculations

<u>Carbon-14</u> makes up about 1/10 000 000 (one <u>ten-millionth</u>) of the carbon in the <u>air</u>. This level stays <u>fairly constant</u> in the <u>atmosphere</u>. The same proportion of C-14 is also found in <u>living things</u>. However, when they <u>die</u>, the C-14 is <u>trapped inside</u> the wood or wool or whatever, and it <u>gradually decays</u> with a <u>half-life</u> of <u>5730 years</u>. By simply measuring the <u>proportion</u> of C-14 found in some old <u>axe handle</u>, <u>burial shroud</u>, etc. you can easily calculate <u>how long ago</u> the item was <u>living material</u> using the known <u>half-life</u>.

<u>EXAMPLE:</u> An axe handle was found to contain 1 part in 40 000 000 carbon-14. How old is the axe?

<u>ANSWER:</u> The C-14 was originally <u>1 part in 10 000 000</u>. After <u>one half-life</u> it would be down to <u>1 part in 20 000 000</u>. After <u>two half-lives</u> it would be down to <u>1 part in 40 000 000</u>. Hence the axe handle is <u>two C-14 half-lives</u> old, i.e. $2 \times 5730 = $ <u>11 460 years old</u>.

Note the same old <u>stepwise method</u> from page 58, going down one half-life at a time.

Dating Rocks — Relative Proportions Calculations

<u>Uranium isotopes</u> have <u>very long half-lives</u> and decay via a <u>series</u> of short-lived particles to produce <u>stable isotopes of lead</u>. The <u>relative proportions</u> of uranium and lead isotopes in a sample of <u>igneous rock</u> can therefore be used to <u>date</u> the rock, using the <u>known half-life</u> of the uranium. It's as simple as this:

Initially	After one half-life	After two half-lives
100% uranium	50% uranium	25% uranium
0% lead	50% lead	75% lead

Ratio of uranium to lead:	(half-life of uranium-238 = 4.5 billion years)	
Initially	After one half-life	After two half-lives
1:0	1:1	1:3

Will any of that be in your exam? — isotope so...

So, not just Sellafield. Amazing how many uses there are for radioactive materials — not all bad either.

Nuclear Power

Nuclear Fission — The Splitting Up of Uranium Atoms

<u>Nuclear power stations</u> are powered by <u>nuclear reactors</u>. In a nuclear reactor, a controlled <u>chain reaction</u> takes place in which uranium or plutonium atoms <u>split up</u> and <u>release energy</u> in the form of <u>heat</u>. This heat is then used to <u>heat water</u> to drive a <u>steam turbine</u>. So nuclear reactors are really just <u>glorified steam engines</u>!

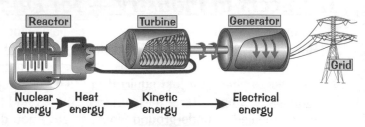

The Splitting of Uranium-235 Needs Neutrons

<u>Uranium-235</u> (i.e. a uranium atom with a total of 235 protons and neutrons) is used in some <u>nuclear reactors</u> (and <u>bombs</u> — a nuclear bomb is an <u>uncontrolled</u> fission reaction).

1) Uranium-235 (U-235) is actually quite <u>stable</u>, so it needs to be <u>made unstable</u> before it'll split.
2) This is done by firing <u>slow-moving neutrons</u> at the U-235 atom.
3) The neutron joins the nucleus to create <u>U-236</u>, which is <u>unstable</u>.
4) The U-236 then <u>splits</u> into two smaller atoms, plus 2 or 3 <u>fast-moving</u> neutrons.
5) There are <u>different</u> pairs of atoms that U-236 can split into — e.g. krypton-90 and barium-144, which are <u>radioactive</u>.

You Can Split More than One Atom — Chain Reactions

1) To get a useful amount of energy, loads of U-235 atoms have to be split. So neutrons released from **previous** fissions are used to hit **other** U-235 atoms.
2) These cause **more** atoms to **split**, releasing **even more** neutrons, which hit **even more** U-235 atoms... and so on and so on. This process is known as a **chain reaction**.
3) The **fission** of an atom of uranium releases **loads** of **energy**, in the form of the **kinetic energy** of the two new atoms (which is basically **heat**).

Inside a Gas-Cooled Nuclear Reactor

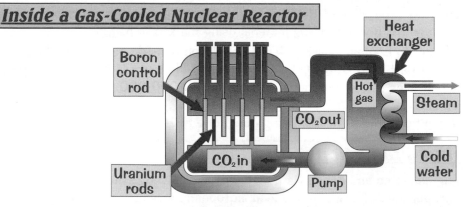

This is a <u>gas-cooled</u> nuclear reactor — but there are many other kinds.

1) <u>Free neutrons</u> in the reactor "<u>kick-start</u>" the fission process.
2) The two <u>fission fragments</u> then <u>collide</u> with surrounding atoms, causing the <u>temperature</u> in the reactor to <u>rise</u>.
3) <u>Control rods</u>, often made of <u>boron</u>, limit the rate of fission by <u>absorbing</u> excess neutrons.
4) A gas, typically <u>carbon dioxide</u>, is pumped through the <u>reactor</u> in order to carry away the <u>heat</u> generated.
5) The gas is then passed through the <u>heat exchanger</u>, where it gives its energy to <u>water</u>. This water is heated and turned into <u>steam</u>, which is then used to turn the <u>turbines</u>, generating electricity.

Uranium — gone fission, back after lunch...

The products left over after nuclear fission are generally <u>radioactive</u>, so they can't just be thrown away. Sometimes they're put in <u>thick metal boxes</u>, which are then placed in a <u>deep hole</u>, which is then filled with <u>concrete</u>. But some people worry that the materials could leak out after a number of years. Hmm.

Revision Summary for Module P4

Some of this stuff can be just learnt and regurgitated — other parts actually need thinking about.
It doesn't help that you can't see most of it happening — you'll just have to take my word for it.
If you can answer these questions, you should have no problem with anything the examiners throw at you.
But if any of these questions stump you, go back and learn the stuff, then give it another go.

1) What is static electricity? What causes it to build up?

2) Which particles move when static builds up? Which particles don't move?

3) Give two examples each of static electricity being: a) a nuisance, b) dangerous.

4) Explain how you can reduce the danger of getting a static electric shock.

5) Give three examples of how static electricity can be helpful. Write all the details.

6) Explain what current, voltage and resistance are in an electric circuit.

7) Sketch a properly wired three-pin plug.

8) Explain fully how fuses work.

9) Describe what earthing and double insulation are. Why are they useful?

10) A variable resistor is used to change the resistance in a circuit. What happens to the current flowing through a circuit if the resistance is increased?

11) Explain how you could work out the resistance of a resistor.

12) Define the frequency, wavelength and amplitude of a wave.

13) What's the relationship between frequency and pitch in a sound wave?

14) What is ultrasound? Give details of two medical applications of ultrasound.

15) Explain why ultrasound rather than X-rays are used to take images of a foetus.

16) What is the main difference between X-rays and gamma rays?

17) Explain what kind of damage radiation causes to body cells. What are the effects of high doses? What damage do lower doses do?

18) Which kinds of radioactive source are most dangerous: a) inside the body, b) outside the body?

19) Radioactivity is a totally random process. Explain what this means.

20)* Write down the nuclear equation for the alpha decay of: a) $^{234}_{92}U$, b) $^{230}_{90}Th$, and c) $^{226}_{88}Ra$.

21)* Write down the nuclear equation for the beta/gamma decay of: a) $^{234}_{90}Th$, b) $^{234}_{91}Pa$, and c) $^{14}_{6}C$.

22) Sketch a diagram to show how the activity of a radioactive sample decreases over time.

23) Give a proper definition of half-life.

24) Sketch a typical graph of activity against time. Show how you can find the half-life from your graph.

25) List three places where the level of background radiation is increased and explain why.

26) Describe in detail how radioactive sources are used in each of the following:
a) treating cancer, b) tracers in medicine, c) sterilisation.

27) Describe in detail how radioactive sources are used in each of the following:
a) tracers in industry, b) smoke alarms, c) dating archaeological samples, d) dating rocks.

28)* An old bit of cloth was found to have 1 atom of C-14 to 80 000 000 atoms of C-12. If C-14 decays with a half-life of 5730 yrs, find the age of the cloth.

29) Describe in terms of energy transfers how electricity is produced from a nuclear power station.

30) What type of particle is U-235 bombarded with to make it split?

31) Explain how a chain reaction is created in a nuclear reactor.

32) What is used in a reactor to slow down neutrons which are moving too quickly?

* Answers on page 100.

Module P4 — Radiation for Life

Satellites

A <u>satellite</u> is any object that <u>orbits</u> around a <u>larger object</u> in space. There are natural satellites, like <u>moons</u>, but this page just looks at the artificial ones that we put there ourselves, like for <u>satellite phones</u> and stuff.

Satellites are Set Up by Humans for Many Different Purposes:

1) Monitoring <u>weather</u> and climate.
2) <u>Communications</u>, e.g. phone and TV.
3) <u>Space research</u>, such as the Hubble Telescope.
4) <u>Spying</u> on baddies.
5) <u>Navigation</u>, e.g. the Global Positioning System (GPS).

There are <u>two main kinds of orbit</u> useful for satellites:

1) Communications Satellites Stay Over the Same Point on Earth

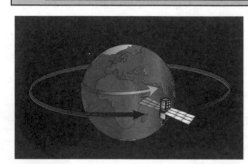

1) Communications satellites are put in <u>quite a high orbit</u> over the <u>equator</u> which takes <u>exactly 24 hours</u> to complete.

2) This means that they <u>stay above the same point</u> on the Earth's surface because the Earth <u>rotates with them</u>.

3) So they're called geostationary satellites (geo(Earth)-stationary) or <u>geosynchronous</u> satellites.

4) They're <u>ideal</u> for <u>telephone</u> and <u>TV</u> because they're always in the <u>same place</u> and can <u>transfer signals</u> from one side of the Earth to another in a <u>fraction of a second</u>.

5) There is room for about <u>400</u> geostationary satellites — any more and their signals will <u>interfere</u>.

2) Weather and Spying Satellites Need to be in a Low Orbit

1) Geostationary satellites are <u>too high</u> and <u>too stationary</u> to take good <u>weather</u> or <u>spying photos</u> — for this you need <u>low polar orbits</u>, which... wait for it... pass over both <u>poles</u> and are <u>nice and low</u>.

2) In a <u>low polar orbit</u>, the satellite sweeps over <u>both poles</u> whilst the Earth <u>rotates beneath it</u>.

3) The time taken for each full orbit is just <u>a few hours</u>. They're much <u>closer</u> to the Earth than geostationary satellites, so the pull of <u>gravity</u> is stronger and they <u>move much faster</u>.

4) Each time the satellite comes round it can <u>scan</u> the next bit of the globe. This allows the <u>whole surface</u> of the planet to be <u>monitored</u> each day.

GPS Satellites and Space Telescopes are in Other Stable Orbits

There are satellites in different stable orbits from those above, such as <u>GPS (Global Positioning System)</u> satellites and the <u>Hubble Space Telescope</u>.
But happily you don't need to know anything more about them. Hurrah.

So you can thank satellites next time you ring home from Everest...

In case you're wondering... a GPS system works by transmitting its position and the time. These signals are received by GPS devices in cars or whatever, and once four signals have been received, the device can work out its exact location. It's all clever stuff. And you don't need to learn it, which is even better.

Gravity and Orbits

Gravity attracts all masses, but you only notice it when one of the masses is really really big, like a planet. Anything near a planet or star is attracted to it very strongly. This has three important effects:

1) It makes all things accelerate towards the ground with the same acceleration (≈ 10 m/s^2 on Earth).

2) It gives everything a weight.

3) It keeps planets, moons and other satellites in their orbits:

Gravity Provides the Centripetal Force That Causes Orbits

1) If an object is travelling in a circle it is constantly changing direction, which means there must be a force acting on it (see p27).

2) An orbit is a balance between the forward motion of the object and a force pulling it inwards. This is called a centripetal force (pronounced sen-tree-pee-tal) — it's directed towards the centre of the circle.

3) The planets move around the Sun in almost circular orbits. The centripetal forces that make this happen are provided by the gravity between each planet and the Sun.

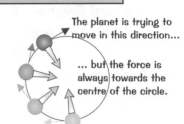

The planet is trying to move in this direction...

... but the force is always towards the centre of the circle.

Gravity Decreases Quickly as You Get Further Away

1) With very large masses like stars and planets, gravity is very big and acts a long way out.

2) The closer you get to a star or a planet, the stronger the force of attraction.

3) Because of this stronger force, planets nearer the Sun move faster and cover their orbit quicker.

4) Moons, artificial satellites and space stations are also held in orbit by gravity. The further out from Earth they orbit, the slower they move (see page 64 for more on satellites).

5) The size of the force due to gravity follows the fairly famous "inverse square" relationship. The main effect of that is that the force decreases very quickly with increasing distance. The formula is $F \propto 1/d^2$, but I reckon it's easier just to remember the basic idea in words:

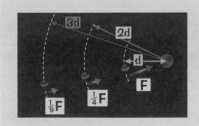

a) If you double the distance from a planet, the size of the force will decrease by a factor of four (2^2).

b) If you treble the distance, the force of gravity will decrease by a factor of nine (3^2), and so on.

c) On the other hand, if you get twice as close the gravity becomes four times stronger.

That's Why Comets Speed Up and Slow Down...

1) Comets orbit the Sun, but have very eccentric (elongated) orbits.

2) The Sun isn't at the centre of the orbit but near one end, so their orbits take them out a long way from the Sun, then back in close again.

3) The comet travels much faster when it's nearer the Sun than it does in the more distant parts of its orbit. That's because the increased pull of gravity makes it speed up the closer it gets to the Sun.

Comet

Gravity — all my troubles seemed so far away...

So satellites keep the world in touch, and gravity keeps the satellites orbiting so that they can do their many and various jobs. And gravity of course is also what keeps us whizzing round the Sun, without which we'd be a bit scuppered. But that's another story.

Speed and Velocity

When you're talking about the motion of a car, it's <u>not enough</u> just to talk about its <u>speed</u>. Sure, I'm driving at <u>30 mph</u>, but <u>which way</u> am I going? Am I heading <u>towards that tree</u> over there or not? And that lorry over there is also going at 30 mph — but is it heading towards me? And am I getting paranoid?

Speed is Just a Number, but Velocity Has Direction Too

1) To measure the <u>speed</u> of an object, you only need to measure <u>how fast</u> it's going — the <u>direction</u> is <u>not important</u>. E.g. speed = 30 mph.

2) <u>Velocity</u> is a <u>more useful</u> measure of <u>motion</u>, because it describes both the <u>speed and direction</u>. E.g. velocity = 30 mph due north.

3) A quantity like <u>speed</u>, that has only a <u>number</u>, is called a <u>scalar</u> quantity. A quantity like <u>velocity</u>, that has a <u>direction as well</u>, is a <u>vector</u> quantity.

<u>Scalar quantities:</u>
mass, temperature, time, length, etc.

<u>Vector quantities:</u>
force, displacement, acceleration, momentum, etc.

All speeds = 0.5 m/s
Velocities = completely different

You Can Calculate Average Speed to Get the Overall Picture

1) <u>Speed</u> is a measure of <u>how fast</u> an object is moving at any given <u>moment</u>, but during a journey, your speed can <u>change</u>. For example, if I drove from Birmingham to London, I might drive at 30 miles per hour leaving Birmingham, then get up to 70 mph on the motorway, then slow down to 2 mph to find a parking place in London.

2) You know that speed = distance ÷ time (see p34). Likewise you can calculate the <u>average speed</u> of a journey, where the <u>distance</u> is the <u>total distance</u> covered, and <u>time</u> is the <u>total time</u> taken for the journey:

$$\text{average speed} = \frac{\text{total distance}}{\text{total time}}$$

E.g. a walker covers 600 m in 375 s. His average speed is 600 m ÷ 375 s = 1.6 m/s... but he'll probably have gone faster or slower than that at different times during the walk.

Relative Speed Compares the Speeds of Two Different Objects

1) When you look out of a <u>car window</u>, a car that's <u>overtaking</u> you looks like it's <u>not moving very fast</u>. Whereas a car on the <u>opposite side</u> of the motorway seems to <u>whizz past</u> at 100 miles an hour.

2) It's all to do with <u>relative speed</u> — how fast something's going <u>relative to something else</u>. The easiest way to think of it is to imagine yourself in a moving car, watching another vehicle from the window.

3) A car going the <u>same way</u> as you will only have a small speed <u>relative to your car</u>...

→ 30 mph

EXAMPLE

40 mph, or 10 mph relative to car 1

...whereas a car going the <u>opposite way</u> will have a much <u>bigger</u> speed <u>relative to you</u>.

→ 30 mph

EXAMPLE

← 40 mph, or 70 mph relative to car 3

My speed relative to Michael Schumacher is — well, slower...

You could do an <u>experiment</u> in the lab to find relative speeds. Put a ticker tape machine on a trolley, and attach the ticker tape to a toy car. Depending on whether the <u>car and trolley</u> are moving in the <u>same</u> or <u>opposite directions</u>, you'd get different results. Good excuse to put the books down for a bit, anyway.

Combining Velocities and Forces

If a parrot has the <u>wind behind it</u>, it flies a bit <u>faster</u>. Likewise, if it's flying <u>into the wind</u>, it'll be slower. To work out the velocity as seen by a "<u>stationary observer</u>" (someone <u>standing still</u>), you have to <u>combine</u> the <u>velocity of the parrot</u> with the <u>velocity of the wind</u>. Get ready for a bit of <u>maths</u> — this is vector stuff...

To Combine Two Vectors, You Add Them End to End

1) With or Against the Current — EASY

It's <u>easy</u> when the plane (or whatever) is flying <u>directly into the wind</u> (or whatever), or with the <u>wind behind it</u>. On the vector diagrams you just need arrows going back and forwards, like this:

EXAMPLE: A light plane is flying east. Its airspeed indicator shows 120 km/h. It is flying into a wind of 20 km/h — i.e. within a stream of air that's moving west at 20 km/h. What is its resultant velocity?

Draw the vectors <u>end to end</u>:

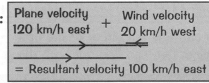

Plane velocity
120 km/h east + Wind velocity
20 km/h west

= Resultant velocity 100 km/h east

→ Plane Velocity
← Wind Velocity

So an observer on the ground would see the plane going <u>east at 100 km/h</u>.

2) Across the Current — A Bit More Maths

If the <u>plane</u> (or whatever) is flying <u>across the wind</u> (or whatever), it's a bit <u>more tricky</u>.

→ Plane Velocity
Wind Velocity

EXAMPLE: A boat is going west at 14 m/s (according to the speed indicator) in a river with a current running north at 8 m/s. What is its resultant velocity?

Again, you draw the vectors <u>end to end</u>, only this time it makes a triangle:

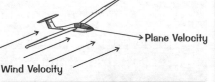

Current velocity
8 m/s north

Resultant velocity

θ

Boat velocity
14 m/s west

To work out the resultant velocity, you need both speed and direction. It's a right-angled triangle, so:

For <u>speed</u> you need <u>Pythagoras</u>' theorem: speed = $\sqrt{(8^2 + 14^2)}$ = <u>16.1 m/s</u>

And for <u>direction</u>, it's good old <u>trigonometry</u>:   tan θ = 8/14, so θ = tan⁻¹ (8/14) = <u>29.7°</u>

It's the Same with Forces and ANY Vectors at Right Angles

EXAMPLE: Two big <u>beasties</u> pulling a boat along a canal, with forces at <u>right angles</u> to each other.

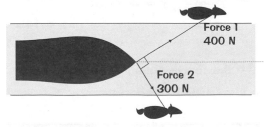

Force 1
400 N

Force 2
300 N

Force 1
400 N

Force 2
300 N

θ

Resultant Force

Draw the vectors <u>end to end</u>, to make a right-angled triangle:

And it's Pythagoras again:

Size of Force = $\sqrt{(300^2 + 400^2)}$ = <u>500 N</u>

Direction = angle of θ to Force 1, which you find by trig:

tan θ = 300/400, so θ = tan⁻¹ (3/4) = <u>36.9°</u>

I've got a brand new combine velocity...

You use the same trick to combine <u>any vectors</u> — momentum, displacement, acceleration, anything. Just draw the vectors end to end and, with a bit of maths, you can find the overall (resultant) vector.

Equations of Motion

These <u>equations of motion</u> are dead handy for working out <u>velocity</u>, <u>acceleration</u> and other goodies...

You Need to Know These Four Equations of Motion

Which of these equations you need to use depends on what you <u>already know</u>, and what you need to <u>find out</u>. But that means you have to know all four equations — preferably like the back of your hand.

Altogether, there are <u>5 things</u> involved in these equations:

<u>u</u> = <u>initial velocity</u>,   <u>t</u> = <u>time</u>,
<u>v</u> = <u>final velocity</u>,   <u>a</u> = <u>acceleration</u>.
<u>s</u> = <u>displacement</u>,

$$s = \frac{(u+v)}{2}t \qquad v = u + at$$

$$s = ut + \frac{1}{2}at^2 \qquad v^2 = u^2 + 2as$$

Make Sure You Use the Right Equation

If you know <u>three things</u>, you can find out <u>either</u> of the <u>other two</u> — if you use the <u>right equation</u>, that is. And if you use this method <u>twice</u>, you can find out <u>both</u> things you don't know.

HOW TO CHOOSE YOUR EQUATION:

1) Write down which <u>three</u> things you <u>already know</u>.
2) Write down <u>which</u> of the other things you want to <u>find out</u>.
3) <u>Choose</u> the equation that involves <u>all</u> the things you've <u>written down</u>.
4) <u>Stick in</u> your numbers, and do the <u>maths</u>.

REMEMBER:
Direction's important for <u>velocity</u>, <u>acceleration</u> & <u>displacement</u> — always choose which direction's <u>positive</u>, and <u>stick</u> with it.

EXAMPLE: A car going at 10 m/s accelerates at 2 m/s² for 8 s. How far does the car go while accelerating?

Now, first things first... I'll say that the "<u>positive</u>" direction is "<u>to the right</u>".

1) You know <u>u</u> (= 10 m/s), <u>a</u> (= 2 m/s²) and <u>t</u> (= 8 s).
2) You want to <u>find out</u> the distance, <u>s</u>.
3) So you need the equation with <u>all</u> these in: <u>u</u>, <u>a</u>, <u>t</u> and <u>s</u> — the third equation: $s = ut + \frac{1}{2}at^2$.
4) Put the numbers in: $s = (10 \times 8) + \frac{1}{2}(2 \times 8^2) = 80 + 64 = \underline{144 \text{ m}}$

u = 10 m/s   a = 2 m/s²
t = 8 s
s = ?

EXAMPLE: A car going at 25 m/s decelerates at 1.5 m/s² as it heads towards a built-up area 145 m away. What will its velocity be when it reaches the built-up area?

I'll make the "<u>positive</u>" direction "<u>to the right</u>" again.

1) You know <u>u</u> (= 25 m/s), <u>a</u> (= –1.5 m/s² ...don't forget it's –ve!) and <u>s</u> (= 145 m).
2) You want to <u>find out</u> the final velocity, <u>v</u>.
3) So you need the equation with <u>all</u> these in: <u>u</u>, <u>a</u>, <u>s</u> and <u>v</u> — the fourth equation: v² = u² + 2as.
4) Put the numbers in: $v^2 = 25^2 + 2(-1.5)(145) = 190$ so $v = \sqrt{190} = \underline{13.8 \text{ m/s}}$

u = 25 m/s   a = –1.5 m/s²
s = 145 m
v = ?

Motion problems — eat more figs or follow the method above...

1) <u>LEARN THE EQUATIONS IN THE RED BOXES.</u> You just have to learn them, there's no way round that.
2) <u>LEARN THE METHOD IN THE BLUE BOX.</u> Motion questions can look tricky at first, but that method works for all of them. Practise the examples again — cover up my working and do them yourself.

Projectile Motion

Is it a bird? Is it a plane? No, it's a projectile.

Hmm... exciting stuff, this — things flying through the air, where the only force on them is due to <u>gravity</u>.

The Path of a Projectile is Always a Parabola

1) A <u>projectile</u> is something that is <u>projected</u>, or <u>dropped</u>, and from then on has <u>only gravity</u> acting on it (ignoring air resistance).

2) So things like cannonballs, golf balls, paper darts and long-jumpers are all projectiles.

3) The <u>path</u> a projectile takes through the air (called its <u>trajectory</u>) is always a <u>parabola</u>, which is this shape:

Deal with Horizontal and Vertical Motion Separately

1) Motion can be split into <u>two</u> separate bits — the <u>horizontal</u> bit and the <u>vertical</u> bit.

2) These bits are totally <u>separate</u> — one doesn't affect the other.

3) So gravity (which only acts downwards) <u>doesn't affect horizontal motion at all</u>.

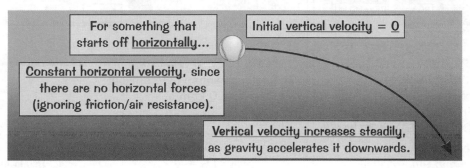

For something that starts off <u>horizontally</u>...

Initial <u>vertical velocity = 0</u>

<u>Constant horizontal velocity</u>, since there are no horizontal forces (ignoring friction/air resistance).

Vertical velocity increases steadily, as gravity accelerates it downwards.

4) Both bits of the motion — the horizontal velocity and the vertical velocity — are <u>vectors</u>. The overall (resultant) velocity of the ball at any point is the <u>vector sum</u> of the separate bits (see p67).

Projectile Calculations Use the Equations of Motion

Example: A football is kicked horizontally from a 20 m high wall. How long is it before it lands? Take g = 10 m/s².

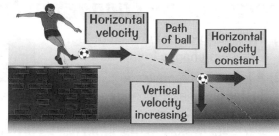

not to scale (otherwise he'd be a very tall man)

It lands when it's travelled 20 m vertically.

Using $s = ut + \frac{1}{2}at^2$, where u = 0, a = 10 m/s², s = 20:

$20 = (0 \times t) + \frac{1}{2}at^2 = \frac{10t^2}{2}$, i.e. <u>t = 2 s</u> when it lands

If its horizontal velocity is originally 5 m/s, how far does it travel before it lands?

Using "distance = speed × time", where v = 5 and t = 2:
    s = 5 × 2 = <u>10 m</u>.

From above.

What do mathematicians do if they have motion problems...?

Get a pencil and, er, draw a diagram. Always start projectiles questions with a diagram. If it doesn't look like you've much info... DON'T PANIC. Remember — if it starts from rest, you know that initial velocity = 0. You also know that if it's moving under gravity, the acceleration is about 10 m/s² downwards.

Momentum

A large rugby player running very fast is going to be a lot harder to stop than a scrawny one out for a Sunday afternoon stroll — that's momentum for you.

Momentum = Mass × Velocity

1) The greater the mass of an object and the greater its velocity, the more momentum the object has.

2) Momentum is a vector quantity — it has size and direction (like velocity, but not speed).

$$\frac{\text{momentum}}{\text{mass} \times \text{velocity}}$$

Momentum (kg m/s) = Mass (kg) × Velocity (m/s)

Momentum Before = Momentum After

When no external forces act, momentum is conserved — i.e. the total momentum after is the same as it was before.

Example 1:

Two skaters approach each other, collide and move off together as shown. At what velocity do they move after the collision?

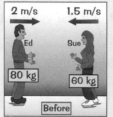

2 m/s   1.5 m/s   Velocity (v) = ?
Ed   Sue
80 kg   60 kg   (80+60) kg
Before   After

1) Choose which direction is positive. I'll say "positive" means "to the right".

2) Total momentum before collision
   = momentum of Ed + momentum of Sue
   = {80 × 2} + {60 × (−1.5)} = 70 kg m/s

3) Total momentum after collision
   = momentum of Ed and Sue together
   = 140 × v

4) So 140v = 70, i.e. v = 0.5 m/s to the right

Example 2:

A gun fires a bullet as shown. At what speed does the gun move backwards?

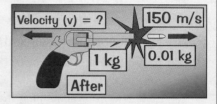

Velocity (v) = ?   150 m/s
1 kg   0.01 kg
After

1) Choose which direction is positive. Again, I reckon "positive" means "to the right".

2) Total momentum before firing
   = 0 kg m/s

3) Total momentum after firing
   = momentum of bullet + momentum of gun
   = (0.01 × 150) + (1 × v)
   = 1.5 + v

This is the gun's recoil.

4) So 1.5 + v = 0, i.e. v = −1.5 m/s
   So the gun moves backwards at 1.5 m/s.

Rockets work in much the same way — they chuck a load of exhaust gases out backwards, and since momentum is conserved, the rocket moves forwards.

Forces Cause Changes in Momentum

1) When a force acts on an object, it causes a change in momentum.

$$\text{Force acting (N)} = \frac{\text{Change in Momentum (kg m/s)}}{\text{Time taken for change to happen (s)}}$$

2) A larger force means a faster change of momentum (and so a greater acceleration).

3) Likewise, if someone's momentum changes very quickly (like in a car crash), the forces on the body will be very large (and more likely to cause injury).

4) This is why cars are designed to slow people down over a longer time when they have a crash — the longer it takes for a change in momentum, the smaller the force.

CRUMPLE ZONES crumple on impact, increasing the time taken for the car to stop.

SEAT BELTS stretch slightly, increasing the time taken for the wearer to stop. This reduces the forces acting on the chest.

AIR BAGS also slow you down more slowly.

Crash test dummies know all too well about momentum...

There's more car safety stuff in Module P3 if you want to have a quick peek. Now then... momentum is always conserved in collisions and explosions (when no external forces act). So momentum before = momentum after. You need to be able to apply that to whatever situation they throw at you in the exam.

Radio Waves and Communication

A long wave <u>radio transmitter</u> sends out a <u>continuous high frequency radio carrier wave</u>.
The <u>signal</u> (e.g. music) is <u>superimposed</u> or <u>encoded</u> on the carrier wave using <u>amplitude modulation</u>:

AM — Amplitude Modulation The <u>sound wave</u>
from the music '<u>modulates</u>' or <u>changes the carrier
wave</u> by <u>changing its amplitude</u>.

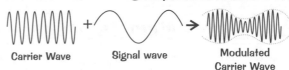

Carrier Wave   Signal wave   Modulated
Carrier Wave

Different Frequency Waves Travel By Different Routes

1) **GROUND WAVES** travel in <u>close contact</u> with the <u>ground</u> as they <u>spread out</u> from the transmitter.
Used by <u>LW/MW radio</u> bands (up to <u>3 MHz</u>). See the bit below (on long wavelength radio waves).

2) **SKY WAVES** Frequencies up to about <u>30 MHz</u> (shortwave radio) can <u>reflect</u> off a layer of the
atmosphere called the <u>ionosphere</u>. This allows the wave to travel longer distances and deals with the
<u>curvature</u> of the Earth. Frequencies <u>above 30 MHz</u> (FM radio and TV) pass straight through the
atmosphere however, and transmissions must be by <u>line of sight</u>.

3) **SPACE WAVES** <u>Microwave</u> signals have a very high
<u>carrier frequency</u> — <u>over 3000 MHz (3 GHz)</u> for
satellite TV and telephones. These <u>pass easily</u> through
the <u>atmosphere</u> and <u>reflect off satellites</u> orbiting the
Earth, enabling the signal to reach <u>distant parts</u> of the
planet. Some satellites are <u>passive</u>, simply <u>reflecting</u>
signal waves that hit them. Others are <u>active</u>, receiving
the signal and <u>retransmitting</u> it.

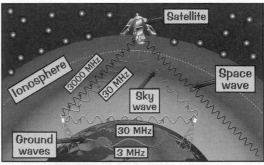

The <u>highest frequency</u> that can be used to carry satellite transmissions is about <u>30 GHz</u>.
Above 30 GHz, <u>rain</u> and <u>dust</u> in the atmosphere <u>absorb</u> and <u>scatter</u> the radio waves.
This <u>reduces the strength</u> of the signal.

Long Wavelength Radio Waves Diffract (There's some stuff on this in P1 as well — see p9.)

1) All waves tend to <u>spread out</u> (diffract) when they pass through a <u>narrow gap</u> or <u>past an object</u>.

2) A "<u>narrow</u>" gap is one which is about the <u>same size</u> as the <u>wavelength</u>.

3) Obviously then, the question of whether a gap is "<u>narrow</u>" or not depends on the <u>wave</u> in question.
What may be a <u>narrow</u> gap for a <u>long wavelength radio wave</u> will be a <u>huge gap</u> for a <u>microwave</u>.

4) It should be obvious then that <u>the longer the wavelength</u> of a wave, <u>the more it will diffract</u>.
You get <u>maximum diffraction</u> when the <u>size of the gap</u> is equal to the <u>wavelength</u> of the wave.

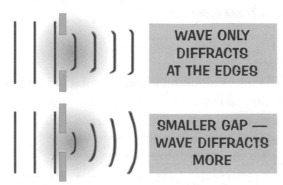

WAVE ONLY
DIFFRACTS
AT THE EDGES

SMALLER GAP —
WAVE DIFFRACTS
MORE

Long Wavelength Radio Waves Diffract Easily over Hills and into Buildings:

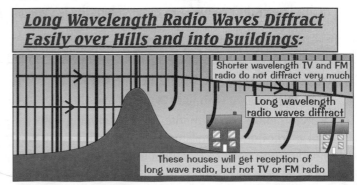

Shorter wavelength TV and FM
radio do not diffract very much

Long wavelength
radio waves diffract

These houses will get reception of
long wave radio, but not TV or FM radio

5) This means long wavelength radio waves have a <u>really long range</u>. They spread out in all directions so
are great for <u>broadcasting</u>, and can diffract <u>over hills</u> and <u>through tunnels</u>, and even <u>over the horizon</u>.

Diffraction — it can drive you round the bend...

And you thought radio was simple — turn it on and Bob's your aardvark. Hmmm... 'fraid not chaps.

Interference of Waves

Waves can interfere with each other, you know. Uh-huh. If you've got two big speakers in a big hall, you can get areas of loud and quiet bits, where the waves have either added to each other or cancelled out.

When Waves Meet They Cause a Disturbance
(just like teenagers)

1) All waves cause some kind of <u>disturbance</u> in a medium — water waves disturb water particles, sound waves disturb air particles, electromagnetic waves disturb electric and magnetic fields.

2) When <u>two waves meet</u> at a point they both try to cause their own disturbance.

3) Waves either disturb in the <u>same direction</u> (<u>constructive</u> interference), or in <u>opposite directions</u> (<u>destructive</u> interference).

4) Think of a '<u>pulse</u>' travelling down a slinky spring meeting a pulse travelling in the opposite direction. These diagrams show the <u>possible outcomes:</u>

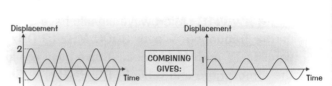

5) The <u>total amplitude</u> of the waves at a point is the <u>sum</u> of the <u>displacements</u> (you have to take direction into account) of the waves at that point.

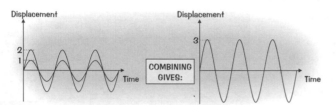

You Get Patterns of 'Loud' and 'Quiet' Bits with Sound

Two speakers both play the same note, starting at <u>exactly</u> the <u>same time</u>, and are arranged as shown:

Depending on where you stand in front of them, you'll either hear a <u>loud sound</u> or <u>almost nothing</u>.

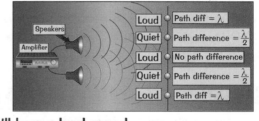

1) At certain points, the sound waves will be <u>in phase</u> — here you get <u>constructive interference</u>. The <u>amplitude</u> of the waves will be <u>doubled</u>, so you'll hear a <u>loud sound</u>.

2) These points occur where the <u>distance travelled</u> by the waves from both speakers is either the <u>same</u> or different by a <u>whole number of wavelengths</u>.

3) At certain other points the sound waves will be exactly <u>out of phase</u> — here you get <u>destructive interference</u> and the waves will <u>cancel out</u>. This means you'll hear almost <u>no sound</u>.

4) These out of phase points occur where the difference in the <u>distance travelled</u> by the waves (the "<u>path difference</u>") is ½ wavelength, 1½ wavelengths, 2½ wavelengths, etc.

Interference of Light Makes 'Bright' and 'Dark' Bits

1) <u>Observing interference</u> effects with <u>light</u> waves is really <u>difficult</u> because their wavelengths are so <u>small</u>. <u>Path differences</u> with light waves have therefore got to be <u>really tiny</u>.

2) A chap called <u>Young</u> managed it by shining light through a pair of <u>narrow slits</u> that were just a <u>fraction of a millimetre</u> apart. This light then hit a screen in a dark room. There was an interference pattern of <u>light bands</u> (constructive) and <u>dark bands</u> (destructive) on the screen.

3) He was able to calculate the <u>wavelength of light</u> and help physicists unravel some of its mysteries...

Destructive interference — too many cooks spoil the wave...

It's weird, isn't it... I mean, constructive interference makes perfect sense — two waves, bigger sound... it's just destructive interference that gets me. I know I've just drawn the diagrams — I know WHY it happens... but I still find it weird. Just one of the Universe's little quirks I suppose. (Like peanut butter.)

Diffraction Patterns and Polarisation

When light <u>diffracts</u> (spreads out through a gap) it also makes an interference pattern — just to confuse everyone. This is a bit tricky, but it's kinda interesting (and useful) so listen up...

When Light Diffracts You Get Patterns of Light and Dark

1) You get <u>interference patterns</u> when waves of <u>equal frequency</u> or <u>wavelength overlap</u> — see page 72.

2) When a wavefront passes through a <u>gap</u>, <u>light</u> from <u>each point</u> along the gap <u>diffracts</u>. It's as if <u>every point along the wavefront is a</u> <u>light source in its own right</u>. Strange but true.

3) <u>Diffracted light</u> from <u>each</u> of these points interferes with light diffracted from all the <u>other points</u>. So you get an <u>interference pattern</u> even from just <u>one slit</u>.

4) The pattern has a <u>bright central fringe</u> with <u>alternating dark and bright fringes</u> on either side of it.

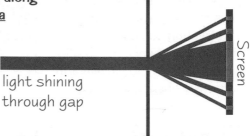

light shining through gap

Screen

EM Waves are Transverse

<u>Most waves</u> are <u>transverse</u>:

1) <u>Light</u> and <u>all other EM waves</u>.

2) <u>Ripples</u> on water.

3) <u>Strings</u> wiggled up and down.

In <u>**TRANSVERSE**</u> waves the vibrations are at <u>90°</u> to the <u>**DIRECTION OF TRAVEL**</u> of the wave.

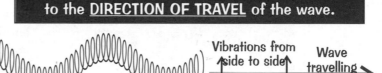

Vibrations from side to side

Wave travelling this way

Transverse Waves Can be Plane Polarised

1) You can make a <u>transverse wave</u> by shaking a rope <u>up and down</u>, or <u>side to side</u>, or in a <u>mixture</u> of directions. Whichever <u>plane</u> you're shaking it in, it's still a transverse wave.

2) Now imagine trying to pass a rope that's waving about in <u>all</u> <u>different directions</u> through the slats of a wooden fence.

3) The only vibrations that'll get through the fence are the <u>vertical</u> ones. The fence <u>filters out</u> vibrations in all the other directions. This is called <u>plane polarisation</u> of the wave.

4) <u>Ordinary light</u> waves are a <u>mixture of vibrations</u> in different directions.

5) Passing the light through a <u>polarising filter</u> is like passing the rope through the fence — the filter only <u>transmits</u> (lets through) vibrations in one particular direction.

6) That means if you have two polarising filters at <u>right angles</u> to each other, then <u>no</u> light can get through.

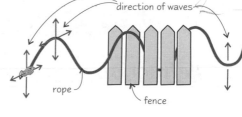

direction of waves

rope

fence

1) <u>Polaroid sunglasses</u> act as polarising filters.

2) When light is <u>reflected</u> from a <u>horizontal surface</u> it is (partly) <u>horizontally polarised</u>.

3) So a <u>vertical polariser</u> can filter out <u>reflected glare</u> from the <u>sea</u> or the <u>snow</u> especially well.

Plane polarised — a tinted windscreen in your cockpit...

So many uses... <u>Windscreens</u> can be made of polarising glass to cut down <u>reflected glare</u> from the road. A photographer might put a polariser over the <u>camera lens</u> to take <u>photos of water</u>. And <u>anglers</u> use <u>Polaroid sunglasses</u> so they can <u>see the fish</u> through the water, instead of being blinded by <u>reflections</u>.

Refraction

1) <u>Refraction</u> is when waves <u>change direction</u> as they <u>enter a different medium</u>.
2) This is caused <u>entirely</u> by the <u>change in speed</u> of the waves.
3) The speed change also causes the <u>wavelength</u> to change, but remember — the <u>frequency doesn't</u> change.

1) Refraction is Shown by Waves in a Ripple Tank Slowing Down

1) The waves travel <u>slower</u> in <u>shallower water</u>, causing <u>refraction</u> as shown.
2) There's a <u>change in direction</u> and a <u>change in wavelength</u>, but <u>NO change in frequency</u>.

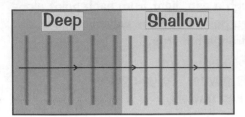
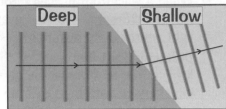

2) Refraction of Light — The Good Old Glass Block Demo

You can't fail to remember the old "<u>ray of light through a rectangular glass block</u>" trick.
Make sure you can draw this diagram <u>from memory</u>, with every detail <u>perfect</u>.

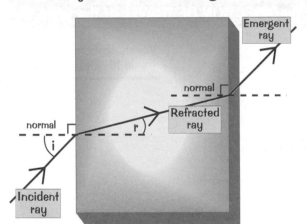

1) <u>Take careful note</u> of the positions of the <u>normals</u> and the <u>exact positions</u> of the angles of <u>incidence</u>, i, and <u>refraction</u>, r (and note it's the angle of <u>refraction</u> — not <u>reflection</u>).

2) Most important of all, remember <u>which way</u> the ray <u>bends</u>.

3) The ray bends <u>towards the normal</u> as it enters the <u>denser medium</u>, and <u>away</u> from the normal as it <u>emerges</u> into the <u>less dense</u> medium.

4) Try to <u>visualise</u> the shape of the <u>wiggle</u> in the diagram — that can be easier than remembering the rule in words.

3) Refraction is Always Caused by the Waves Changing Speed

1) When waves <u>slow down</u> they bend <u>towards</u> the normal.

2) When <u>light</u> enters <u>glass</u> it <u>slows down</u> to about <u>2/3 of its normal speed</u> (in air), i.e. it slows down to about 2×10^8 m/s rather than 3×10^8 m/s.

3) The ratio of the speed of light in a vacuum to the speed of light in a medium is called the <u>refractive index</u> of the medium (3/2 for glass) — see P.76. The <u>higher</u> the <u>refractive index</u>, the <u>more</u> the light <u>bends</u> when it enters or leaves the medium.

4) When waves hit a boundary <u>along the normal</u>, i.e. at <u>exactly 90°</u>, then there will be <u>no change</u> in direction. That's pretty important to remember, because they often <u>sneak it into a question</u> somewhere. There'll still be a change in <u>speed</u> and <u>wavelength</u>, though.

5) <u>Some</u> light is also <u>reflected</u> when it hits a <u>different medium</u>, such as glass.

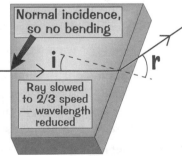

Yay — ripple tanks...

Light slows down when it enters <u>water</u> as well. You know in that game at the fair, where you can win a goldfish if you can drop a penny on top of another penny at the bottom of a bucket of water? You never win, because the penny isn't actually where you think it is. Light from the penny speeds up as it leaves the water, and bends — so the penny looks nearer than it is.

Refraction: Two Special Cases

Dispersion Produces Rainbows

1) Different colours of light are refracted by different amounts.

2) This is because they travel at slightly different speeds in any given medium.

3) A prism can be used to make the different colours of white light emerge at different angles.

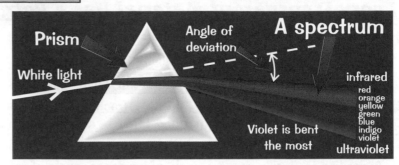

Prism
White light
Angle of deviation
A spectrum
Violet is bent the most
infrared
red
orange
yellow
green
blue
indigo
violet
ultraviolet

4) This produces a spectrum showing all the colours of the rainbow. This effect is called **DISPERSION**.

5) You need to know that red light is refracted the least — and violet is refracted the most.

6) Also know the order of colours in between: Red Orange Yellow Green Blue Indigo Violet
which is remembered by: Richard Of York Gave Battle In Vain
They may well test whether you can put them correctly into the diagram.

7) Also learn where infrared and ultraviolet light would appear if you could detect them.

Total Internal Reflection and the Critical Angle

1) This only happens when light is coming out of something dense like glass or water or perspex.

2) If the angle is shallow enough the ray won't come out at all, but will reflect back into the glass (or whatever). This is called total internal reflection because all of the light reflects back in.

3) You definitely need to learn this set of three diagrams which show the three conditions:

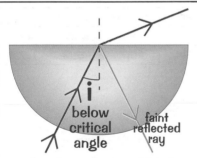

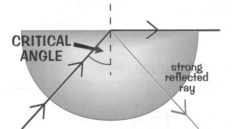

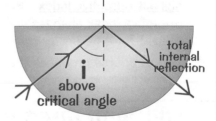

below critical angle
faint reflected ray

CRITICAL ANGLE
strong reflected ray

above critical angle
total internal reflection

Angle of Incidence LESS than the Critical Angle.
Most of the light passes through into the air but a little bit of it is internally reflected.

Angle of Incidence EQUAL TO the Critical Angle.
The emerging ray travels along the surface. There's quite a bit of internal reflection.

Angle of Incidence GREATER than the Critical Angle.
No light comes out. It's all internally reflected, i.e. total internal reflection.

1) The critical angle for glass is about 42°. This is very handy because it means 45° angles can be used to get total internal reflection, as in the prisms in binoculars and periscopes.

2) In diamond the critical angle is much lower — about 24°. That's why diamonds sparkle so much, because there are lots of internal reflections.

3) You can work out critical angles from Snell's law — see next page.

Yay — rainbows and diamonds...

I'm sure you remember doing all about prisms and rainbows in Key Stage 3, but you need more detail for GCSE. You're expected to know **why it happens**, remember **which colour diffracts least** (red) and **most** (violet)... AND be able to **explain dispersion** in terms of **refractive index** (next page)...

Refractive Index and Snell's Law

So you're totally happy with the last 2 pages. And you're sure about that. Good. Gets a bit hairy here...

Every Transparent Material Has a Refractive Index

1) The absolute refractive index of a material is defined as:

$$\text{refractive index, } n = \frac{\text{speed of light in a vacuum, c}}{\text{speed of light in that material, v}}$$

$$n = \frac{c}{v}$$

(speed of light in a vacuum, $c = 3 \times 10^8$ m/s)

2) Light <u>slows down a lot</u> in <u>glass</u>, so the <u>refractive index</u> of glass is <u>high</u> (around 1.5). The refractive index of <u>water</u> is a bit <u>lower</u> (around 1.33) — so light doesn't slow down as much in water as in glass.

3) The <u>speed of light in air</u> is about the <u>same</u> as in a <u>vacuum</u>, so the <u>refractive index</u> of <u>air</u> is 1 (to 2 d.p.).

4) According to Snell's law, the <u>angle of incidence</u>, <u>angle of refraction</u> and <u>refractive index</u> are all <u>linked</u>...

Snell's Law Says...

<u>When an incident ray passes into a material</u>:

$$n = \frac{\sin i}{\sin r}$$

So if you know <u>any two</u> of <u>n</u>, <u>i</u> or <u>r</u>, you can work out the <u>missing one</u>.

(Thankfully you don't have to know <u>why</u> Snell's law works. Just that it does.)

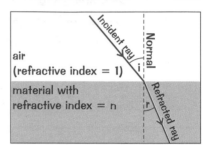

air (refractive index = 1)

material with refractive index = n

Refractive Index Explains Dispersion...

1) <u>Refractive index</u> of a medium is the <u>ratio</u> of speed of light in a vacuum to speed of light in that medium.

2) So any material has a <u>different refractive index</u> for each <u>different speed of light</u>.

3) <u>Red</u> light <u>slows down</u> the <u>least</u> when it travels from air into glass, so it is refracted the least and has the <u>lowest refractive index</u>. <u>Violet light</u> has the <u>highest refractive index</u>. Here's how the refractive index changes with the wavelength of light for a particular type of glass:

colour of light	red	yellow	blue	violet
wavelength (in nm)	656	589	486	434
refractive index of glass	1.514	1.517	1.523	1.528

4) This of course produces the famous <u>dispersion</u> effect — see p75.
(Same with rainbows — they're due to the different refractive indexes of water for different colours.)

...and Total Internal Reflection

1) When light leaves a material with <u>higher refractive index</u> and enters a material with a <u>lower refractive index</u>, it <u>speeds up</u> and so bends <u>away from the normal</u> — e.g. when travelling from <u>glass into air</u>.

2) If you keep <u>increasing</u> the <u>angle of incidence</u>, the <u>angle of refraction</u> gets closer and closer to <u>90°</u>. Eventually i reaches a <u>critical angle</u> C for which <u>r = 90°</u>. The light is refracted right along the <u>boundary</u>. Above this critical angle, you get <u>total internal reflection</u> — no light leaves the medium.

r = 90°

Critical angle, C

total internal reflection

i more than C

3) You can find the <u>critical angle</u>, C, using this equation:

$$\sin C = \frac{n_r}{n_i}$$

n_r is the <u>refractive index</u> of the stuff the light's travelling <u>TOWARDS</u>.

n_i is the <u>refractive index</u> of the material the light starts <u>FROM</u>.

4) The <u>higher the refractive index</u>, the <u>lower the critical angle</u>. For water, C is 49°, and for glass it's 42°.

Well — at least it's only 3 formulas to learn...

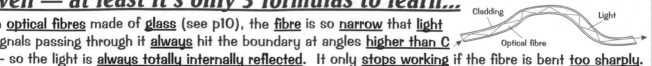

In <u>optical fibres</u> made of <u>glass</u> (see p10), the <u>fibre</u> is so <u>narrow</u> that <u>light</u> signals passing through it <u>always</u> hit the boundary at angles <u>higher than C</u> — so the light is <u>always totally internally reflected</u>. It only <u>stops working</u> if the fibre is bent <u>too sharply</u>.

Cladding   Light
Optical fibre

Images and Converging Lenses

<u>Lenses</u> are usually made of <u>glass or plastic</u>. All lenses change the <u>direction of rays</u> of light by <u>refraction</u> — light <u>slows down</u> when it enters the lens and <u>speeds up</u> when it leaves, causing it to bend.

A Real Image is Actually There — A Virtual Image is Not

1) A <u>real image</u> is where the <u>light from an object</u> comes together to form an <u>image on a 'screen'</u> — like the image formed on an eye's <u>retina</u> (the 'screen' at the back of an <u>eye</u>).

2) A <u>virtual image</u> is when the rays are diverging, so the light from the object <u>appears</u> to be coming from a completely <u>different place</u>.

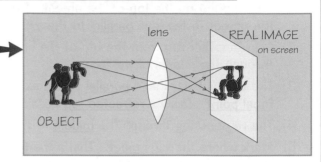

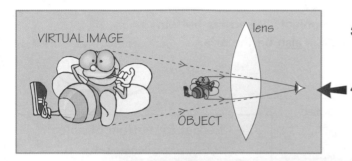

3) When you look in a <u>mirror</u> you see a <u>virtual image</u> of your face — the <u>object</u> (your face) <u>appears</u> to be <u>behind the mirror</u>.

4) You can get a virtual image when looking at an object through a <u>magnifying lens</u> — the virtual image looks <u>bigger</u> and <u>further away</u> than the object <u>actually</u> is.

To describe an image properly, you need to say <u>4 things</u>:

1) <u>How big it is</u> compared to the object;

2) Whether it's <u>upright</u> or <u>inverted</u> (upside down);

3) Whether it's <u>real or virtual</u>.

4) <u>Where it is</u> (in relation to the lens and the focal points).

Converging Lenses Focus Light

1) A <u>converging</u> lens is <u>convex</u> — it <u>bulges outwards</u>. It causes rays of <u>light</u> to converge (move <u>together</u>) to a <u>focus</u>.

2) If the rays entering the lens are <u>parallel</u> to each other and to the <u>axis</u>, it focuses them at a point called the <u>focal point</u>.

3) The distance between the centre of the lens and the focal point is called the <u>focal length</u> of the lens.

4) Converging lenses work the other way round too — they can turn <u>diverging light rays</u> into <u>parallel light</u>.

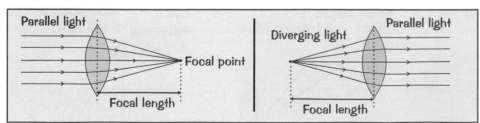

5) Converging lenses can make <u>real or virtual</u> images, depending on <u>how close</u> the object is to the lens.

Important stuff this — come on, focus focus...

So you get an exam question: "Bob looks through a magnifying glass at a beetle one focal length away from the lens. Describe the image he sees." **How many things do you need to say about the image in your answer... is it one? Nope. Two? Wrong again. Three? Um, no. Four? Yep, got it.**

Ray Diagrams

Ray diagrams are those fiddly pictures you draw to work out what the image through a lens looks like. And guess what... you'll probably have to draw one in the exam.

Draw a Ray Diagram to Show the Image From a Converging Lens

1) Pick a point on the **top** of the object. Draw a ray going from the object to the lens **parallel** to the axis of the lens.

2) Draw another ray from the top of the object going right through the middle of the lens.

3) The incident ray that's **parallel** to the axis is **refracted** through the **focal point**. Draw a **refracted ray** passing through the **focal point**.

4) The ray passing through the **middle** of the lens doesn't bend.

5) Mark where the rays **meet**. That's the **top of the image**.

6) Repeat the process for a point on the bottom of the object. When the bottom of the object is on the **axis**, the bottom of the image is **also** on the axis.

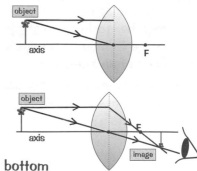

EXAMPLE:

1) and 2) — draw incident rays from top of object:

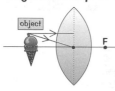

3), 4), 5) — draw refracted rays to find top of image:

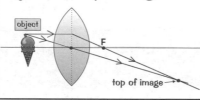

6) — Repeat for bottom of object:

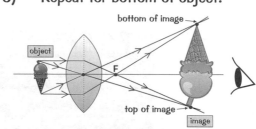

If you **really** want to be sure, you can draw a third incident ray.
Draw a line from the top of the object, passing through the focal point in front of the lens. Refract it so that it leaves the lens parallel to the axis.
In the exam you can get away with just two rays, so you only need bother with the third if you want to double-check.

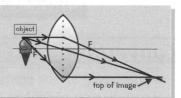

Distance from the Lens Affects the Image

1) An object **at 2F** will produce a **real**, **upside down** image the **same size** as the object, and **at 2F**.

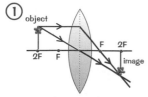

2) **Between F and 2F** it'll make a **real**, **upside down** image **bigger** than the object, and **beyond 2F**.

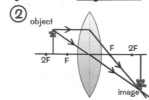

3) An object **nearer than F** will make a **virtual** image the **right way up**, **bigger** than the object and on the **same side** of the lens.

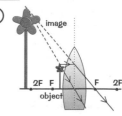

👤 ← **Ray...**

Ray diagrams. Hmm, not the easiest things in the world. But to be frank, the **method's** pretty **simple** — it's just **drawing them accurately** that people fall down on — one **little mistake** can ruin the **whole thing**. So: **sharp pencil** & **ruler** at the ready. If you draw a line wrong, rub it out and start again. **No excuses**.

Uses — Magnification and Cameras

Converging lenses are used in magnifying glasses and in cameras.

Magnifying Glasses Use Convex Lenses

Magnifying glasses work by creating a magnified virtual image.

1) The object being magnified must be closer to the lens than the focal length (or you get a different kind of image — see diagrams on p78).

2) The image produced is a virtual image. The light rays don't actually come from the place where the image appears to be.

3) Remember "you can't project a virtual image onto a screen" — that's a useful thing to say in the exam if they ask you about virtual images.

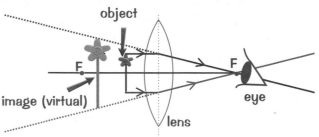

Learn the Magnification Formula

You can use the magnification formula to work out the magnification produced by a lens (or a mirror):

$$\text{Magnification} = \frac{\text{image height}}{\text{object height}}$$

Example: A coin with diameter 14 mm is placed a certain distance behind a magnifying lens. The virtual image produced has a diameter of 35 mm. What is the magnification of the lens at this distance?

magnification = 35 ÷ 14
= 2.5

In the exam you might have to draw a ray diagram to show where an image would be, then measure the image and work out the magnification of the lens. Another reason to draw those ray diagrams carefully...

Taking a Photo Forms an Image on the Film

When you take a photograph of a flower, light from the object (flower) travels to the camera and is refracted by the lens, forming an image on the film.

1) The image on the film is a real image because light rays actually meet there.

2) The image is smaller than the object, because the object's a lot further away than the focal length of the lens.

3) The image is inverted — upside down.

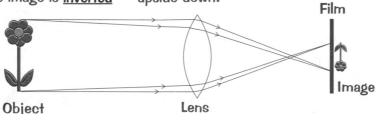

4) The same thing happens in our eye — a real, inverted image forms on the retina. Our very clever brains flip the image so that we see it right way up.

5) In a projector, a lens is used to make a real, inverted, magnified image that forms on a screen.

Picture this — you've revised it, and it turns up on the exam...

They're quite keen on making sure you know what all this physics is actually used for. In this case, it's the joys of magnifying glasses and cameras. Scribble down a quick mini-essay on lenses in magnifying glasses, and one on lenses in cameras. And learn the formula.

Revision Summary for Module P5

Phew. Bit of a mixed bag, that section.

OK, you know what I'm going to say. If you reckon you know your stuff, then do these questions and prove it to yourself. If you can't do these questions now, you won't be able to do them in the exam.

1) Name five uses for artificial satellites.

2) State three differences between a low polar orbit and a geostationary orbit.

3) Gravity is the force of attraction between two masses. What happens to the size of this force if the distance between the masses decreases? Name three important effects of gravity.

4) Two identical satellites orbit at different distances from the Earth. Satellite A orbits the Earth at a distance of 10 000 km and satellite B orbits at 20 000 km. Which satellite has the smaller orbital period? Explain your answer.

5) Explain why comets speed up and slow down during their orbits.

6) What's the difference between speed and velocity? Give an example of each.

7)* A tractor travels 2 miles along farm tracks, and it takes 15 minutes. It then travels a further 10 miles on a country road, and this part of the journey takes 30 minutes. Calculate the tractor's average speed for the whole journey in miles per hour.

8)* A boat is sailing due south with a velocity of 0.5 m/s relative to the water. The river is flowing at 0.2 m/s due north. Draw a vector diagram to help find the boat's resultant velocity.

9)* A bird is facing due north and flying at 12 mph relative to the air. There is a 5 mph wind blowing due west. Draw a vector diagram to help find the resultant velocity of the bird.

10)* Find the distance travelled by a soggy pea as it is flicked from rest to a speed of 14 m/s in 0.4 s.   (assume constant acceleration)

11) What shape is the trajectory (path) of a projectile?

12)* A sandwich is thrown horizontally off a skyscraper at 1.5 m/s. It hits the ground 10 s later.
a) How high is the skyscraper? Take g = 10 m/s²   (ignoring air resistance)
b) How far will the sandwich have travelled horizontally before it hits the ground?

13)* Write down the formula for momentum. Find the momentum of a 78 kg sheep falling at 15 m/s.

14) If the total momentum of a system before a collision is zero, what is the total momentum of the system after the collision?

15)* A gymnast (mass 50 kg) jumps off a beam and hits the floor at a speed of 7 m/s. She bends her knees and stops moving in 0.5 s. What is the average force acting on her?

16) Explain how air bags, seat belts and crumple zones reduce the risk of serious injury in a car crash.

17) Describe the differences between ground waves, sky waves and space waves.

18) What is diffraction? Which will diffract more easily over hills, long or short wavelength radio waves?

19) Draw wave diagrams to show the difference between constructive and destructive interference. Describe the effect of interference of waves in the context of: a) sound, b) light.

20) What effect does a polarising filter have on the light passing through it? What would happen if you had two polarising filters over a light source, at right angles to each other?

21) Draw a diagram to show the path of a ray of light as it passes from:
air → rectangular block of glass → air, meeting the block of glass at an angle.

22) Write down the formula for refractive index, in words. For which colour light does glass have the highest refractive index — violet, green or red?

23)* Write down the Snell's law formula. A beam of light enters a material with i = 30°. It bends so that r = 20°. What is the refractive index of the material?

24) What is a real image? How is it different from a virtual image?

25) Copy and complete this ray diagram to show the image formed:

26)* Peter measures the length of a seed to be 1.5 cm. When he looks at the seed through a converging lens at a certain distance, the seed appears to have a length of 4.5 cm. What is the magnification of this lens at this distance?

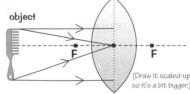

object

(Draw it scaled-up so it's a bit bigger.)

* Answers on p100.

Module P5 — Space for Reflection

Circuits — The Basics

Isn't electricity great — hair straighteners, computers, life-support machines... Mind you it's pretty bad news if the technical terms don't mean anything to you. Probably best to get them learnt.

1) **Current** is the flow of electrons round the circuit.
Current will only flow through a component if there is a voltage across that component.
Current is measured in amps, A.

2) **Voltage** is the driving force that pushes the current round.
Kind of like "electrical pressure".
Voltage is measured in volts, V.

3) **Resistance** is anything in the circuit which slows the flow down — it's measured in ohms, Ω. (Ω is the Greek letter omega.)

4) **There's a Balance:** the voltage is trying to push the current round the circuit, and the resistance is opposing it — the relative sizes of the voltage and resistance decide how big the current will be:

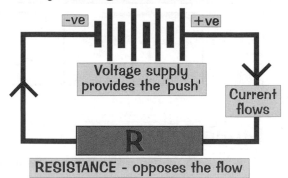

If you increase the voltage — then more current will flow.
If you increase the resistance — then less current will flow
(or more voltage will be needed to keep the same current flowing).

The Standard Test Circuit

This is without doubt the most totally bog-standard circuit the world has ever known. So know it.

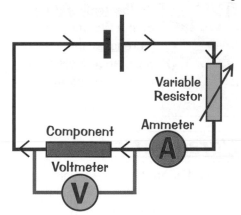

The Ammeter

1) Measures the current flowing through the component.
2) Must be placed in series.
3) Can be put anywhere in series in the main circuit, but never in parallel like the voltmeter.

The Voltmeter

1) Measures the voltage across the component.
2) Must be placed in parallel around the component under test — **NOT** around the variable resistor or the battery!
3) The proper name for voltage is "potential difference" or "P.D.".

Five Important Points

1) This very basic circuit is used for testing components, and for getting V-I graphs for them (see p82).
2) The component, the ammeter and the variable resistor are all in series, which means they can be put in any order in the main circuit. The voltmeter, on the other hand, can only be placed in parallel around the component under test, as shown. Anywhere else is a definite no-no.
3) As you vary the variable resistor it alters the current flowing through the circuit.
4) This allows you to take several pairs of readings from the ammeter and voltmeter.
5) You can then plot these values for current and voltage on a V-I graph.

Measure gymnastics — use a vaultmeter...

This page is all about electric circuits — what they are, how to use them, and how they work. This is some of the most basic stuff on electricity there is. I assume you realise that you'll never be able to learn anything else about electricity in circuits until you know this stuff — don't you? Good-oh.

Voltage-Current Graphs and Resistance

Learn These Circuit Symbols

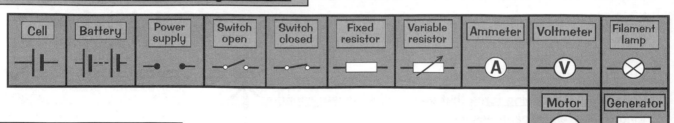

| Cell | Battery | Power supply | Switch open | Switch closed | Fixed resistor | Variable resistor | Ammeter | Voltmeter | Filament lamp |

| Motor | Generator |

Variable Resistor

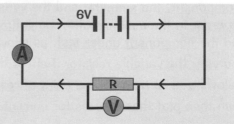

1) A <u>resistor</u> whose resistance can be <u>changed</u> by twiddling a knob or something.

2) The old-fashioned ones were huge coils of <u>wire</u> with a <u>sliding contact</u> to <u>change the length</u> of <u>resistive wire</u> in the circuit.

3) They're great for <u>altering</u> the current flowing through a circuit. Turn the resistance <u>up</u>, the current <u>drops</u>. Turn the resistance <u>down</u>, the current goes <u>up</u>. <u>Increasing</u> the current makes <u>bulbs brighter</u> and <u>motors spin faster</u>.

4) They're used to control things like the <u>volume</u> of a CD player or the <u>speed</u> of a food processor.

Hideously Important Voltage-Current Graphs

V-I graphs show how the current varies as you change the voltage. Learn these two really well:

Different Resistors

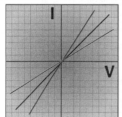

The current through a <u>resistor</u> (at constant temperature) is <u>proportional to voltage</u>. <u>Different resistors</u> have different <u>resistances</u>, hence the different <u>slopes</u>.

Filament Lamp

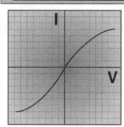

As the <u>temperature</u> of the filament <u>increases</u>, the <u>resistance increases</u>, hence the <u>curve</u>.

Calculating Resistance: R = V/I (or R = "1/gradient")

For the <u>straight-line graphs</u>, the resistance of the component is <u>steady</u> and is equal to the <u>inverse</u> of the <u>gradient</u> of the line, or "<u>1/gradient</u>". In other words, the <u>steeper</u> the graph the <u>lower</u> the resistance. If the graph <u>curves</u>, it means the resistance is <u>changing</u>. In that case R can be found for any point by taking the <u>pair of values</u> (V, I) from the graph and sticking them in the formula <u>R = V/I</u>.

$$\text{Resistance} = \frac{\text{Potential Difference}}{\text{Current}}$$

$$\frac{V}{I \times R}$$

EXAMPLE:
Voltmeter V reads 6 V across a resistor R of 4 Ω.
What is the current through ammeter A?

ANSWER. Use the formula $V = I \times R$.
We need to find I, so the version we need is $I = \frac{V}{R}$.
The answer is then $\frac{6}{4}$, which is 1.5 A.

Voltage-current graphs — also more fun than gravel... (see p.35)

You have to be able to <u>interpret</u> voltage-current graphs for your exam. Remember — the <u>steeper</u> the <u>slope</u>, the <u>lower</u> the <u>resistance</u>. And you need to know that equation inside out, back to front, upside down and in Swahili. It's the most important equation in electrics, bar none. (P.S. I might let you off the Swahili.)

Potential Dividers

Potential dividers consist of a pair of resistors. They divide the potential in a circuit so you can get outputs of different voltages.

The Higher the Resistance, the Greater the Voltage Drop

A voltage across a pair of resistors is 'shared out' according to their relative resistances. The rule is:

The larger the share of the total resistance, the larger the share of the total voltage.

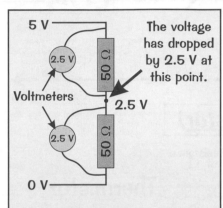

Voltmeters

The voltage has dropped by 2.5 V at this point.

The resistances are equal, so each resistor takes half the voltage.

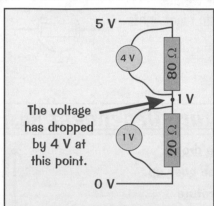

The voltage has dropped by 4 V at this point.

The top resistor has 80% of the total resistance, and so takes 80% of the total voltage.

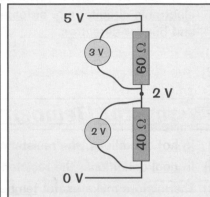

The top resistor has 60% of the total resistance, and so takes 60% of the total voltage.

The point between the two resistors is the 'output' of the potential divider.
This 'output' voltage can be varied by swapping one of the resistors for a variable resistor.

Potential Dividers are Quite Useful

Potential dividers are not only spectacularly interesting — they're useful as well.
They allow you to run a device that requires a certain voltage from a battery of a different voltage.
This is the formula you need to use:

$$V_{out} = V_{in} \times \left(\frac{R_2}{R_1 + R_2} \right)$$

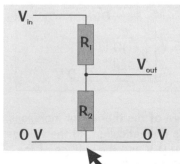

EXAMPLE:
In the diagram, the input voltage for the potential divider is 9 V. R_1 is 20 Ω and R_2 is 40 Ω. What is the output voltage across R_2?

ANSWER:
$$V_{out} = 9\,V \times \left(\frac{40}{20 + 40} \right) = \frac{9\,V \times 40}{60} = 6\,V$$

A potential divider like this could be used to run a 6 V device from a 9 V battery. You could replace one of the resistors by a variable resistor, so that you could change V_{out} to any value between 0 and 9 volts.

My boyfriend's mother is a potential divider...

You're not going to believe this, but potential dividers get even more exciting on the next page. I know what you're thinking — you're worried that your body won't be able to cope with the adrenaline rush. It's just something you have to get used to with Physics, I'm afraid.

LDRs and Thermistors

Some resistors <u>change</u> their resistance depending on the <u>conditions</u>.
You need to know about two of them — <u>light-dependent resistors</u> and <u>thermistors</u>.

Light-Dependent Resistor (or "LDR" to Thee and Me)

1) In <u>bright light</u>, the resistance <u>falls</u>.

2) In <u>darkness</u>, the resistance is <u>highest</u>.

3) This makes it a useful device for various <u>electronic circuits</u>, e.g. <u>automatic night lights</u> and <u>burglar detectors</u>.

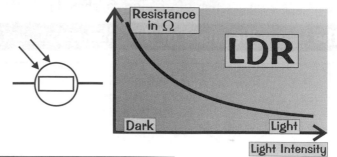

Thermistor (Temperature-Dependent Resistor)

1) In <u>hot</u> conditions, the resistance <u>drops</u>.

2) In <u>cool</u> conditions, the resistance goes <u>up</u>.

3) Thermistors make useful <u>temperature sensors</u>, e.g. <u>car engine</u> temperature gauges and electronic <u>thermostats</u>.

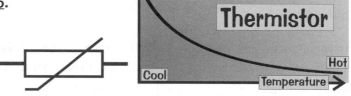

A Thermistor in a Potential Divider Makes a Temperature Sensor

1) Using a <u>thermistor</u> and a <u>variable resistor</u> in a potential divider, you can make a <u>temperature sensor</u> that triggers an output device at a temperature <u>you choose</u>.

2) You can make a temperature sensor that gives a <u>high voltage output</u> (a 'logical 1' — see page 94) when it's hot and a <u>low voltage output</u> (a 'logical 0') when it's cold. This is how it works...

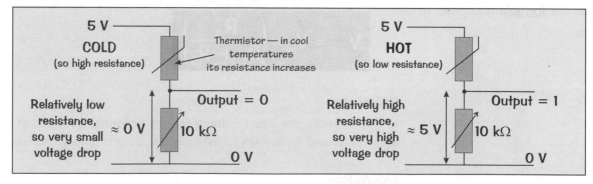

 When the thermistor's <u>cold</u> its resistance is <u>very high</u>, so the voltage drop across it is <u>almost 5 V</u>, meaning the voltage of the output is <u>nearly 0 V</u> — a 'logical 0'.

 As the temperature of the thermistor <u>increases</u>, its resistance <u>falls</u> dramatically. So the voltage across it is <u>almost 0 V</u> and the voltage of the output is <u>nearly 5 V</u> — a 'logical 1'.

3) You can play around with that circuit to make <u>different kinds of sensor</u>. For example, you could use a similar circuit to make a <u>light sensor</u> — just replace the thermistor with an <u>LDR</u>.

How can this stuff be light-dependent if it's so dull...

Okay, when I said "exciting" on the last page, I... um... lied. Sooooo, moving on. Thermistors are used in computers as well. When you first turn the power on, the thermistor's cold, so its resistance is high. The high resistance prevents a surge in the current that could damage a silicon chip. Clever.

Magnetic Fields

Loads of electrical appliances use <u>magnetic fields</u> generated by <u>electric currents</u>.

> A <u>MAGNETIC FIELD</u> is a region where <u>MAGNETIC MATERIALS</u> (like iron and steel) and also <u>WIRES CARRYING CURRENTS</u> experience a <u>FORCE</u> acting on them.

Magnetic fields can be represented by <u>field diagrams</u>.
<u>The arrows on the field lines always point</u> FROM THE NORTH POLE of the magnet TO THE SOUTH POLE.

A Current-Carrying Wire Creates a Magnetic Field

There is a magnetic field around a <u>straight</u>, <u>current-carrying wire</u>.

The field is made up of <u>concentric circles</u> with the wire in the centre.

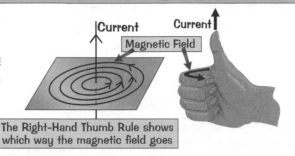

The Right-Hand Thumb Rule shows which way the magnetic field goes

A Rectangular Coil Reinforces the Magnetic Field

1) If you bend the current-carrying wire round into a <u>coil</u>, the magnetic field looks like this.
2) The circular magnetic fields around the sides of the loop <u>reinforce</u> each other at the centre.
3) If the coil has lots of turns, the magnetic fields from all the individual loops <u>reinforce</u> each other even more.

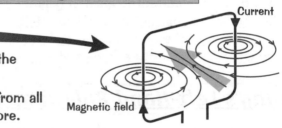

The Magnetic Field Round a Solenoid

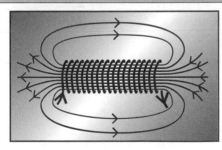

1) The magnetic field <u>inside</u> a current-carrying <u>solenoid</u> (a coil of wire) is <u>strong</u> and <u>uniform</u>.
2) <u>Outside</u> the coil, the field is just like the one round a <u>bar magnet</u>.
3) This means that the <u>ends</u> of a solenoid act like the <u>north pole</u> and <u>south pole</u> of a bar magnet.
4) Pretty obviously, if the <u>direction</u> of the <u>current</u> is <u>reversed</u>, the N and S poles will <u>swap ends</u>.

5) If you imagine looking directly into one end of a solenoid, the <u>direction of current flow</u> tells you whether it's the <u>N or S pole</u> you're looking at, as shown by the <u>two diagrams</u> opposite.
6) You can increase the <u>strength</u> of the magnetic field around a solenoid by adding a magnetically "<u>soft</u>" iron core through the middle of the coil. It's then called an <u>ELECTROMAGNET</u>.

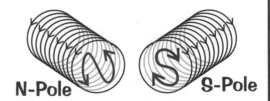

N-Pole   S-Pole

A <u>magnetically soft</u> material <u>magnetises</u> and <u>demagnetises</u> very easily. So, as soon as you <u>turn off</u> the current through the solenoid, the magnetic field <u>disappears</u> — the iron doesn't stay magnetised.

Current-carrying wires always get the thumbs up from me...

...and it's always my <u>RIGHT</u> thumb. Got that? <u>Not</u> my left, but my <u>RIGHT</u> thumb. <u>Don't get them mixed up</u>. You'll use your left hand on the next page, though, so it shouldn't feel too left out... (pun intended)

The Motor Effect

If you put a current-carrying wire into a magnetic field, you have <u>two magnetic fields combining</u>, which puts a force on the wire. The force can make the wire move — which can be quite handy, really.

A Current in a Magnetic Field Experiences a Force

When a current-carrying wire is put between magnetic poles, the two <u>magnetic fields</u> affect one another. The result is a <u>force</u> on the wire.

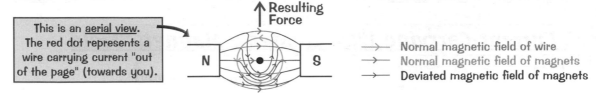

This is an <u>aerial view</u>. The red dot represents a wire carrying current "out of the page" (towards you).

↑ Resulting Force

N   S

→ Normal magnetic field of wire
→ Normal magnetic field of magnets
→ Deviated magnetic field of magnets

1) To experience the <u>full force</u>, the <u>wire</u> has to be at <u>90°</u> to the <u>magnetic field</u>. If the wire runs <u>along</u> the <u>magnetic field</u>, it won't experience <u>any force at all</u>. At angles in between, it'll feel <u>some</u> force.

2) The <u>force</u> gets <u>bigger</u> if either the <u>current</u> or the <u>magnetic field</u> is made bigger.

3) The force always acts in the <u>same direction</u> relative to the <u>magnetic field</u> of the magnets and the <u>direction of the current</u> in the wire.

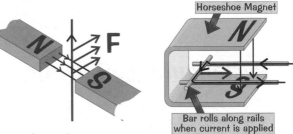

4) A good way of showing the direction of the force is to apply a current to a set of <u>rails</u> inside a <u>horseshoe magnet</u> (shown opposite). A bar is placed on the rails, which <u>completes the circuit</u>. This generates a <u>force</u> that <u>rolls the bar</u> along the rails.

Horseshoe Magnet

Bar rolls along rails when current is applied

Fleming's Left-Hand Rule Tells You Which Way the Force Acts

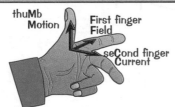

thuMb Motion   First finger Field   seCond finger Current

1) They could test if you can do this, so <u>practise it</u>.

2) Using your <u>left hand</u>, point your <u>First finger</u> in the direction of the <u>Field</u> and your <u>seCond finger</u> in the direction of the <u>Current</u>.

3) Your <u>thuMb</u> will then point in the direction of the <u>force</u> (Motion).

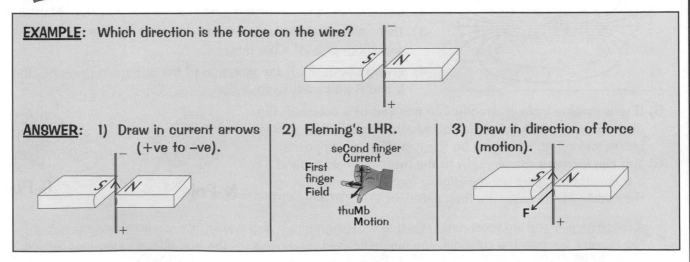

<u>EXAMPLE:</u> Which direction is the force on the wire?

S   N

<u>ANSWER:</u>

1) Draw in current arrows (+ve to –ve).

S   N

2) Fleming's LHR.

seCond finger Current
First finger Field
thuMb Motion

3) Draw in direction of force (motion).

S   N
F

Remember the Left-Hand Rule for Motors — drive on the left...

See, I told you you'd need your left hand for this page. Learn the rule and <u>use it</u> — don't be scared of looking like a muppet in the exam. <u>Learn all the details</u>, diagrams and all, then cover the page and scribble it all down from memory. Then check back, see what you've missed, and try again.

The Simple Electric Motor

Aha — one of the favourite exam topics of all time. Read it. Understand it. Learn it.

The Simple Electric Motor

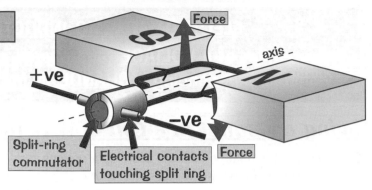

4 Factors which Speed it up
1) More <u>CURRENT</u>
2) More <u>TURNS</u> on the coil
3) <u>STRONGER MAGNETIC FIELD</u>
4) A <u>SOFT IRON CORE</u> in the coil

Split-ring commutator

Electrical contacts touching split ring

1) The diagram shows the <u>forces</u> acting on the two <u>side arms</u> of the <u>coil</u>.
2) These forces are just the <u>usual forces</u> which act on <u>any current</u> in a <u>magnetic field</u>.
3) Because the coil is on a <u>spindle</u> and the forces act <u>one up</u> and <u>one down</u>, it <u>rotates</u>.
4) The <u>split-ring commutator</u> is a clever way of "<u>swapping</u> the contacts <u>every half turn</u> to keep the motor rotating in the <u>same direction</u>". (Learn that statement because they might ask you.)
5) The direction of the motor can be <u>reversed</u> either by swapping the <u>polarity</u> of the <u>DC supply</u> or swapping the <u>magnetic poles</u> over.

EXAMPLE: Is the coil turning clockwise or anticlockwise?

ANSWER:

1) Draw in current arrows (+ve to –ve).

2) Fleming's LHR on one arm (I've used the right-hand arm).

SeCond finger Current

First finger Field

thuMb Motion

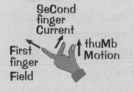

3) Draw in direction of force (motion).

F↑

So — the coil is turning <u>anticlockwise</u>.

Practical Motors Have Pole Pieces Which are Very Curved

1) Link the coil to an <u>axle</u>, and the axle <u>spins round</u>.
2) If you can make your motor powerful enough, that axle can turn just about anything.
3) The problem is that the type of motor shown in the diagram at the top of the page is pretty useless. It's too <u>inefficient</u> to power anything big and heavy.

Curved pole pieces of magnet

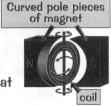

coil

4) Instead, practical motors use <u>pole pieces</u> which are <u>so curved</u> that they form a <u>hollow cylinder</u>. The coil spins inside the cylinder.

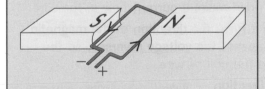

axle

fan

In this diagram there's a <u>fan</u> attached to the axle, but you can stick <u>almost anything</u> on a motor axle and make it spin round.
For example, in a <u>food mixer</u>, the axle's attached to a <u>blade</u> or whisks.
In a <u>CD player</u> the axle's attached to the bit you <u>sit the CD on</u>.

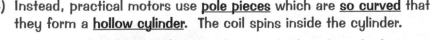

Hello Motor...

<u>Loudspeakers</u> demonstrate the <u>motor effect</u>. <u>AC electrical signals</u> from the <u>amplifier</u> are fed to the <u>speaker coil</u> (shown red). These make the coil move <u>back and forth</u> over the poles of the <u>magnet</u>. These movements make the <u>cardboard cone vibrate</u> and this creates <u>sounds</u>.

Electromagnetic Induction

Electricity is generated using electromagnetic induction. Sounds terrifying, but it isn't that complicated:

> ## ELECTROMAGNETIC INDUCTION:
> The creation of a **VOLTAGE** (and maybe current) in a wire which is experiencing a **CHANGE IN MAGNETIC FIELD**.

(You'll sometimes hear it called the "dynamo effect".)

Moving a Magnet in a Coil of Wire Induces a Voltage

1) <u>Electromagnetic induction</u> means creating a <u>voltage</u> (and maybe a <u>current</u>) in a conductor. You can do this by <u>moving a magnet</u> in a <u>coil of wire</u> or moving a conductor in a magnetic field ("cutting" magnetic field lines). Shifting the magnet from <u>side to side</u> creates a little "<u>blip</u>" of current.

A few examples of electromagnetic induction:

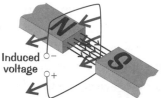
Induced voltage ○− ○+

2) If you move the magnet in the <u>opposite direction</u>, then the <u>voltage/current</u> will be <u>reversed</u> too. Likewise if the <u>polarity</u> of the magnet is <u>reversed</u>, then the <u>voltage/current</u> will be <u>reversed</u> too.

3) If you keep the <u>magnet</u> (or the <u>coil</u>) moving <u>backwards and forwards</u>, you produce a <u>voltage</u> that <u>keeps swapping direction</u> — and this is how you produce <u>AC current</u>.

You can create the same effect by <u>turning</u> a magnet <u>end to end</u> in a coil, to create a current that lasts as long as you spin the magnet. This is how generators work (see next page).

1) As you <u>turn</u> the magnet, the <u>magnetic field</u> through the <u>coil</u> changes — this <u>change</u> in the magnetic field induces a <u>voltage</u>, which can make a <u>current</u> flow in the wire.

2) When you've turned the magnet through half a turn, the <u>direction</u> of the <u>magnetic field</u> through the coil <u>reverses</u>. When this happens, the <u>voltage reverses</u>, so the <u>current</u> flows in the <u>opposite direction</u> around the coil of wire.

3) If you keep turning the magnet in the <u>same direction</u> — always clockwise, say — then the voltage will keep on reversing every half turn and you'll get an <u>AC current</u>.

Four Factors Affect the Size of the Induced Voltage

1) If you want a <u>bigger</u> peak voltage (and current) you have to <u>increase</u> at least one of these four things:

> 1) The **STRENGTH** of the **MAGNET**   2) The **AREA** of the **COIL**
> 3) The <u>number of TURNS</u> on the **COIL**   4) The **SPEED** of movement

2) To <u>reduce</u> the voltage, you would <u>reduce</u> one of those factors, obviously.

3) If you <u>turn</u> the magnet <u>faster</u>, you'll get a higher peak voltage, but also a <u>higher frequency</u> — because the magnetic field is reversing more frequently.

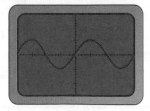

faster turns
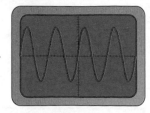

EM Induction — works whether the coil or the field is moving...

"Electromagnetic Induction" gets my vote for "Definitely Most Tricky Topic". If it wasn't so important maybe you wouldn't have to bother learning it. The trouble is, this is how all our electricity is generated.

Generators

Think about the simple electric <u>motor</u> — you've got a current in the wire and a magnetic field, which causes movement. Well, a <u>generator</u> works the <u>opposite way round</u> — you've got a magnetic field and movement, which <u>induces a current</u>.

AC Generators — Just Turn the Coil and There's a Current

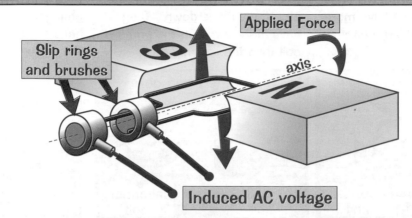

1) Generators <u>rotate a coil</u> in a <u>magnetic field</u> (or a magnet in a coil... see below).

2) Their <u>construction</u> is pretty much like a <u>motor</u>.

3) As the <u>coil spins</u>, a <u>current</u> is <u>induced</u> in the coil. This current <u>changes direction</u> every half turn.

4) Instead of a <u>split-ring commutator</u>, AC generators have <u>slip rings</u> and <u>brushes</u> so the contacts <u>don't swap</u> every half turn.

5) This means they produce <u>AC voltage</u>, as shown by these <u>CRO displays</u>. Note that <u>faster revolutions</u> produce not only <u>more peaks</u> but <u>higher overall voltage</u> too.

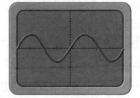

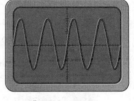

original   faster revs

Dynamos — You Turn the Magnet Instead of the Coil

1) <u>Dynamos</u> are a slightly different type of <u>generator</u>. They rotate the <u>magnet</u> instead of the coil.

2) This still causes the <u>field through the coil</u> to <u>swap</u> every half turn, so the output is <u>just the same</u> as for a generator.

3) This means you get the <u>same CRO traces</u> of course.

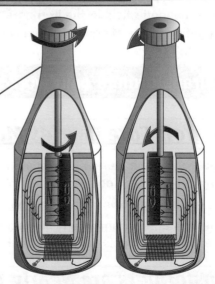

<u>Dynamos</u> are sometimes used on <u>bikes</u> to power the <u>lights</u>. The <u>cog wheel</u> at the top is moved so that it <u>touches</u> one of the <u>bike wheels</u>. As the wheel moves round, it <u>turns</u> the cog which is attached to the <u>magnet</u>. This creates an <u>AC current</u> to power the lights.

Dynamo Kiev — they like a bit of squad rotation...

The National Grid is fed by hundreds of <u>generators</u>. These are usually driven by <u>steam turbines</u> (and the steam usually comes from burning things). You can get small portable petrol generators too, to use where there's no mains electricity — on building sites, say.

Transformers

Transformers use electromagnetic induction to connect two circuits together. Transformers mean that one circuit can power another circuit with a different voltage and current.

There are Three Types of Transformer

STEP-UP TRANSFORMERS step the voltage up. They have **more** turns on the **secondary** coil than the primary coil.

STEP-DOWN TRANSFORMERS step the voltage **down**. They have more turns on the **primary** coil than the secondary.

ISOLATING TRANSFORMERS **don't** change the voltage at all. They have the **same number** of turns on the primary and secondary coils.

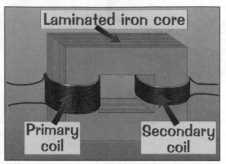

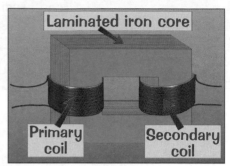

Transformers Work by Electromagnetic Induction

1) The primary coil produces a magnetic field which stays within the iron core. This means nearly all of it passes through the secondary coil and hardly any is lost.

2) Because there is alternating current (AC) in the primary coil, the field in the iron core is constantly changing direction (100 times a second if it's at 50 Hz) — i.e. it is a changing magnetic field.

3) This rapidly changing magnetic field is then felt by the secondary coil.

4) The changing field induces an alternating voltage in the secondary coil (with the same frequency as the alternating current in the primary) — electromagnetic induction of a voltage in fact.

5) The relative number of turns on the two coils determines whether the voltage induced in the secondary coil is greater or less than the voltage in the primary.

6) If you supplied DC to the primary, you'd get nothing out of the secondary at all. Sure, there'd still be a magnetic field in the iron core, but it wouldn't be constantly changing, so there'd be no induction in the secondary because you need a changing field to induce a voltage. Don't you! So don't forget it:

Transformers only work with AC. They won't work with DC at all.

The Iron Core Carries Magnetic Field, Not Current

1) The iron core is purely for transferring the changing magnetic field from the primary coil to the secondary.

2) No electricity flows round the iron core.

3) The iron core is laminated with layers of insulation to reduce eddy currents in the iron. Eddy currents are little 'whirlpools' of charge that build up in the iron, heating it up, and therefore wasting energy.

Transformers are Nearly 100% Efficient So "Power In = Power Out"

The formula for power supplied is: **Power = Voltage × Current** or: **P = V × I**.

So you can rewrite power in = power out as: $$V_p I_p = V_s I_s$$

V_p = primary voltage V_s = secondary voltage
I_p = primary current I_s = secondary current

Transformers

The <u>ratio</u> between the primary and secondary <u>voltages</u> is the same as the <u>ratio</u> between the <u>number of turns</u> on the primary and secondary coils. You can either learn it that way, or learn the formula below.

The Transformer Equation — Use it Either Way Up

You can calculate the output voltage from a transformer if you know the input voltage and the number of turns on each coil.

$$\frac{\text{Primary Voltage}}{\text{Secondary Voltage}} = \frac{\text{Number of turns on Primary}}{\text{Number of turns on Secondary}}$$

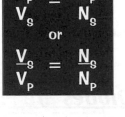

$$\frac{V_P}{V_S} = \frac{N_P}{N_S}$$

or

$$\frac{V_S}{V_P} = \frac{N_S}{N_P}$$

Well, it's <u>just another formula</u>. You stick in the numbers <u>you've got</u> and work out the one <u>that's left</u>. It's really useful to remember you can write it <u>either way up</u> — this example's much trickier algebra-wise if you start with V_s on the bottom...

EXAMPLE: A transformer has 40 turns on the primary and 800 on the secondary. If the input voltage is 1000 V, find the output voltage.

ANSWER: $\frac{V_s}{V_p} = \frac{N_s}{N_p}$, so $\frac{V_s}{1000} = \frac{800}{40}$. $V_s = 1000 \times \frac{800}{40} = \underline{20\ 000\ V}$

Or you can say that 800 is 20 times 40, so the secondary voltage will also be 20 times the primary voltage.

Transformers Are Used on the National Grid

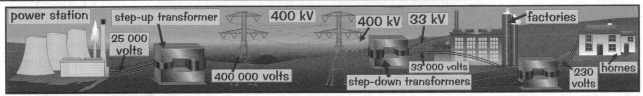

You get both step-up and step-down transformers on the National Grid:

1) To transmit <u>a lot of power</u>, you either need <u>high voltage</u> or <u>high current</u> (P = VI).
2) The problem with <u>high current</u> is the <u>loss</u> (as heat) due to the <u>resistance</u> of the cables.
3) The formula for <u>power loss</u> due to resistance in the cables is: $P = I^2R$.
4) Because of the I^2 bit, if the current is <u>10 times</u> bigger, the losses will be <u>100 times</u> bigger.
5) It's much <u>cheaper</u> to boost the voltage up to <u>400 000 V</u> and keep the current <u>very low</u>.
6) This requires <u>transformers</u> as well as <u>big pylons</u> with <u>huge insulators</u>, but it's still <u>cheaper</u>.
7) The transformers have to <u>step</u> the voltage <u>up</u> at one end, for <u>efficient transmission</u>, and then bring it back down to <u>safe, useable levels</u> at the other end.

Isolating Transformers are Used in Bathrooms

1) Most household transformers <u>reduce</u> the mains voltage for use in <u>low-voltage</u> devices such as radios.
2) However, <u>isolating</u> transformers have <u>equal</u> primary and secondary voltages. That means they have <u>equal numbers of turns</u> on the primary and secondary coils. This is because the only purpose of an isolating transformer is <u>safety</u>.
3) The <u>danger</u> of the <u>mains</u> circuit is that it's connected to the <u>earth</u>, so if you <u>touch</u> the <u>live parts</u> and are <u>also touching the ground</u>, you will <u>complete a circuit</u> with you in it. <u>NOT good</u>.
4) The isolating transformer inside the shaver socket allows you to use the shaver without being <u>physically connected</u> to the mains. So it minimises the risk of the <u>live</u> parts <u>touching</u> the <u>earth</u> lead and likewise <u>minimises your risk</u> of getting <u>electrocuted</u>. Phew.

National Grid — heaven for noughts and crosses fans...

In most power stations, <u>fuels</u> are burned (or uranium is split) and the energy from this powers a massive <u>generator</u>. Not all the heat can be converted into mechanical power, though, so heat is often <u>lost</u> to the environment. If the plant <u>is</u> able to reuse the heat, it's referred to as a <u>cogeneration power plant</u>.

Diodes and Rectification

Mains electricity supplies alternating current (AC), but many devices need direct current (DC). So we need a way of turning AC into DC. That's where diodes come in.

Diodes Only Let Current Flow in One Direction

1) Diodes only let current flow freely in **one direction** — there's a very high resistance in the **other** direction.
2) This turns out to be really useful in various **electronic circuits**.
3) You can tell which direction the current flows from the **circuit symbol**. The **triangle** points in the direction of the current.

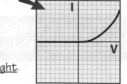

Here the current flows from <u>left to right</u>.

Diodes are Made from Semiconductors Such As Silicon

1) Diodes are often made of **silicon**, which is a **semiconductor**. This means silicon **can** conduct electricity, though not as well as a conductor.
2) Silicon diodes are made from **two different types** of silicon joined together at a 'p-n junction'. One half of the diode is made from silicon that has an impurity added to provide **extra free electrons** — called an **n-type semiconductor** ("n" stands for the "negative" charge of the electrons).
3) A different impurity is added to the other half of the diode so there are **fewer free electrons** than normal. There are lots of **empty spaces** left by these missing electrons which are called **holes**. This type of silicon is called a **p-type semiconductor** ("p" stands for the "positive" charge of the holes).
4) When there's **no potential difference (p.d.)** across the diode, electrons and holes recombine across the two parts of the diode. This creates a **region** where there are **no holes or free electrons**, which acts as an **electrical insulator**.
5) When there is a p.d. across the diode the **direction** is **all-important**:
Applying a p.d. in the **RIGHT direction** means the **free holes and electrons** have **enough energy** to get **across** the **insulating region** to the other side. This means that a **CURRENT FLOWS**.
Applying a p.d. in the **WRONG direction** means the **free holes and electrons** are being **pulled the wrong way**, so they **stay** on the **same side** and **NO CURRENT FLOWS**.

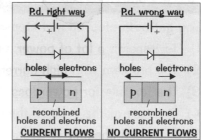

Diodes Can be Used to Rectify AC Current

1) A single diode only lets through current in half of the cycle. This is called **half-wave rectification**.

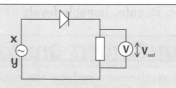

2) To get **full-wave rectification**, you need a **bridge circuit** with four diodes.
In a bridge circuit, the current always flows through the component in the **same direction**, and the output voltage always has the same sign.

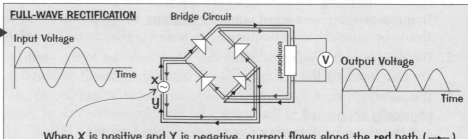

When **X** is positive and **Y** is negative, current flows along the <u>red</u> path (→).
When **Y** is positive and **X** is negative, current flows along the <u>blue</u> path (→).

Yep, it's all just common sense really...

Only joking — this stuff's flippin' hard. At least you've made it through to the other side.

Capacitors

AC voltage that has been rectified is not all that useful in its raw form. Chips are very sensitive to input voltage, and won't work with a voltage that looks like this: ⋀⋀⋀ .
They need a **smoother** voltage like this: ～～～ . This is where **capacitors** come in handy.

Capacitors Store Charge

1) You <u>charge</u> a capacitor by connecting it to a source of voltage, e.g. a battery. A <u>current</u> flows around the circuit, and <u>charge</u> gets <u>stored</u> on the capacitor.

2) The <u>more charge</u> that's stored on a capacitor, the <u>larger the potential difference</u> (or voltage) across it.

3) When the voltage across the capacitor is <u>equal</u> to that of the <u>battery</u>, the <u>current stops</u> and the capacitor is <u>fully charged</u>.

4) The voltage across the capacitor <u>won't rise above</u> the voltage of the battery.

5) If the battery is <u>removed</u>, the capacitor <u>discharges</u>.

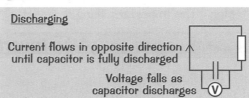

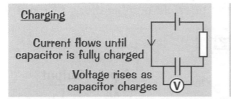

Capacitors are Used in 'Smoothing' Circuits

The output voltage from a rectified AC power supply can be '**smoothed**' by adding a capacitor in **parallel** with the output device. A component gets current **alternately** from the power supply and the capacitor.

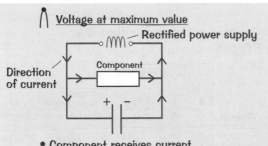

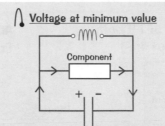

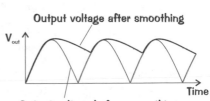

Capacitors are Used to Cause a Time Delay

Capacitors are used in <u>timing circuits</u> and in input sensors that need a <u>delay</u>. Like on a <u>camera</u> when you want to press the button and then run round and get in the shot before the picture's taken.

1) The switch is <u>closed</u>. Initially, the capacitor has <u>no charge</u> stored, and so the voltage drop across it is small. This means the <u>voltage drop</u> across the <u>resistor</u> must be <u>big</u>. (And this all means the <u>output voltage</u> will be low.)

2) As the capacitor <u>charges</u>, the <u>voltage drop</u> across it <u>increases</u> (and so the voltage drop across the resistor <u>falls</u>). This all means the voltage at the output <u>increases</u>.

3) The <u>shutter</u> on the camera will <u>open</u> (i.e. the picture will be taken) when the input is <u>close to 5 V</u>.

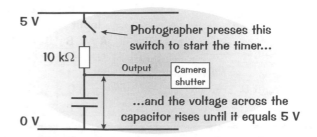

Current never flows through a capacitor...

Capacitors just **store charge**, and then send current back the other way when the voltage falls.

Logic Gates

Learning about <u>logic gates</u> was probably how Bill Gates (no pun intended) got started.
So learn all this stuff, then design a computer operating system that crashes a lot... Bob's your uncle.

Digital Systems are Either On or Off

1) Every connection in a digital system is in one of only <u>two states</u>. It can be either
ON or OFF, either HIGH or LOW, either YES or NO, either 1 or 0... you get the picture.

2) In reality a 1 is a <u>high voltage</u> (about 5 V) and a 0 is a <u>low voltage</u> (about 0 V).
Every part of the system is in one of these two states — nothing in between.

A Logic Gate is a Type of Digital Processor

<u>Logic gates</u> are small, but they're made up of <u>lots</u> of really small components like <u>transistors</u> and <u>resistors</u>.

Each type of logic gate has its own set of <u>rules</u> for converting inputs to outputs, and these rules are best
shown in <u>truth tables</u>. The important thing is to list <u>all</u> the possible <u>combinations</u> of input values.

NOT gate — sometimes called an Inverter

A <u>NOT</u> gate just has <u>one</u> input —
and this input can be either <u>1</u> or <u>0</u>,
so the truth table has just two rows.

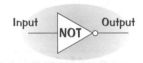

NOT GATE	
Input	Output
0	1
1	0

AND and OR gates usually have Two Inputs

Some AND and OR gates have more than two
inputs, but you don't have to worry about those.

<u>Each input</u> can be 0 or 1, so to allow for <u>all</u> combinations from two inputs, your truth table needs <u>4 rows</u>.
There's a certain logic to the names...

An <u>AND</u> gate only gives an output of 1 if both
the first input <u>AND</u> the second input are 1.

An <u>OR</u> gate just needs either the
first <u>OR</u> the second input to be 1.

AND GATE		
Input		Output
A	B	
0	0	0
0	1	0
1	0	0
1	1	1

OR GATE		
Input		Output
A	B	
0	0	0
0	1	1
1	0	1
1	1	1

You'll quite often see an
OR gate drawn like this:

NAND and NOR gates have the Opposite Output of AND and OR gates

A <u>NAND</u> gate is like <u>combining</u> a <u>NOT</u>
with an <u>AND</u> (hence the name):

If an AND gate would give an output of 0,
a <u>NAND</u> gate would give 1, and vice versa.

A <u>NOR</u> gate is like <u>combining</u> a <u>NOT</u>
with an <u>OR</u> (hence the name):

If an OR gate would give an output of 0,
a <u>NOR</u> gate would give 1, and vice versa.

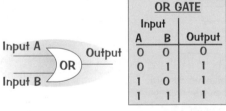

NAND GATE		
Input		Output
A	B	
0	0	1
0	1	1
1	0	1
1	1	0

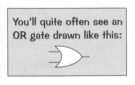

NOR GATE		
Input		Output
A	B	
0	0	1
0	1	0
1	0	0
1	1	0

I like physics, NAND chemistry, NAND biology...

Well at least there aren't that many <u>facts</u> to learn on this page — it's more a question of <u>understanding</u>
the inputs and outputs for the five types of gate. It's a good idea to be familiar with the circuit
symbols of the gates though. And practise writing out those tables — it's the <u>best way</u> to learn.

Using Logic Gates

You need to be able to construct a <u>truth table</u> for a <u>combination</u> of logic gates.
Approach this kind of thing in an <u>organised</u> way and <u>stick to the rules</u>, and you won't go far wrong.

'Interesting' Example — a Greenhouse

Check out the following example — a warning system for a <u>greenhouse</u>. Once the gardener has switched the system on, he wants to be warned if the greenhouse gets <u>too cold</u> or if <u>someone has opened the door</u>.

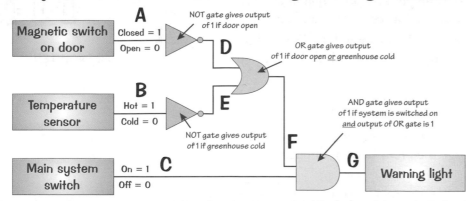

Inputs						Output
A	B	C	D	E	F	G
0	0	0	1	1	1	0
0	0	1	1	1	1	1
0	1	0	1	0	1	0
0	1	1	1	0	1	1
1	0	0	0	1	1	0
1	0	1	0	1	1	1
1	1	0	0	0	0	0
1	1	1	0	0	0	0

The <u>warning light</u> will come on if: (i) it is <u>cold</u> in the greenhouse <u>OR</u> if the <u>door</u> is opened,
(ii) <u>AND</u> the system is switched <u>on</u>.

1) Each connection has a <u>label</u>, and <u>all</u> possible combinations of the inputs are included in the table.
2) What really matters are the <u>inputs</u> and the <u>output</u> — the rest of the truth table is just there to help.

A Latch Works Like a Kind of Memory (but is *really hard* to understand)

1) It's likely that the greenhouse will be too <u>cold</u> in the <u>middle</u> of the night but <u>warm up</u> again by <u>morning</u>. This means the warning light will have <u>gone out</u> by the time the gardener gets out of bed.

2) What the gardener needs is some way of getting the warning light to <u>stay on</u> until it is <u>seen</u> and <u>reset</u>. This is where the <u>latch</u> comes in.

3) A latch can be made by combining two <u>NOR gates</u> as shown. In the above system, the latch would be <u>between</u> the blue <u>OR</u> gate and the green <u>AND</u> gate.

① **When the gardener goes to bed:**
Input F is 0... and output T is 0...
...meaning that the <u>top NOR gate</u> outputs 1...
...and so the <u>bottom NOR gate</u> outputs 0,
    which means... <u>output T</u> remains 0.

② **When the door is opened or the temperature falls:**
Input F becomes 1...
...so <u>output U</u> becomes 0...
...so the <u>bottom NOR gate</u> gives 1
    (as input R is still 0)... i.e. the <u>output</u> is 1.

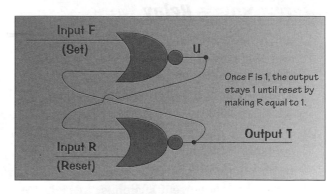

Once F is 1, the output stays 1 until reset by making R equal to 1.

③ **When the door is closed / the temperature rises:**
Input F becomes 0 again...
...but <u>output T</u> is 1 still...
...so <u>output U</u> stays 0 ...and <u>output T</u> stays 1.

④ **To reset the system:**
Briefly make <u>input R</u> equal to 1...
...and since <u>output U</u> is still 0...
...<u>output T</u> becomes 0.

Now we can all sleep easy knowing the cucumbers are safe...

More hard stuff to get your head around here. Try copying out the diagrams of the greenhouse warning system and the latch, and writing in the different inputs. Then follow them through to find the outputs.

LEDs and Relays in Logic Circuits

Two main points on this page: 1) An __LED__ can be used to display the output of a logic gate. 2) Logic gates don't usually supply much current, so they're often connected to a more powerful circuit using a __relay switch__.

LEDs — Light-Emitting Diodes

1) An LED is a __diode__ (see page 92) which __gives out light__.

2) Like other diodes, it only lets current go through in __one direction__. When it does pass current, it gives out a pretty __coloured light__.

3) You can use a light-emitting diode (LED) to show the output of a __logic gate__. If the output is __1__, enough current will flow through the LED to light it up.

4) An LED is a better choice to show output than an ordinary incandescent bulb because it uses __less power__ and __lasts longer__.

5) The LED is often connected in series with a __resistor__ to prevent it from being damaged by too large a current flowing through it.

Circuit symbol for an LED.

A Relay is a Switch Which Connects Two Circuits

1) The __output__ of a logic gate usually allows only a __small current__ to flow through the circuit.

2) But an __output device__ like a motor requires a __large current__.

3) The solution is to have __two circuits__ connected by a __relay__.

4) The relay __isolates__ the __low voltage__ electronic system from the __high voltage__ mains often needed for the __output device__.

There are a few circuit symbols for a relay — this is the simplest one.

5) This also means that it can be made __safer__ for the person __using__ the device — you can make sure that __any parts__ that could come into contact with a __person__ are in the __low-current__ circuit. For example, a __car's starter motor__ needs a very __high current__, but the part __you control__ (when you're turning the key) is in the __low-current circuit__ — __safely isolated__ by the relay.

Here's How a Relay Works...

1) When the switch in the low current circuit is __closed__, it turns on the __electromagnet__ (see page 85), which __attracts__ the __iron contact__ on the __rocker__.

2) The rocker __pivots__ and __closes the contacts__ in the high current circuit — and the motor spins.

3) When the low current switch is __opened__, the electromagnet __stops pulling__, the rocker returns, and the __high current circuit__ is __broken__ again.

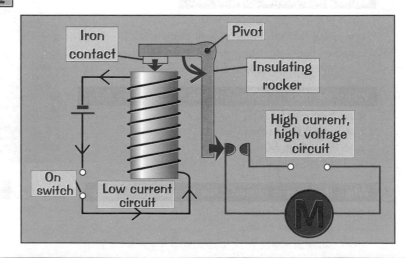

You should now be relay proud of yourself...

...'cos you've completed the whole book. I know Physics isn't always a barrel of laughs. There's a lot of tricky stuff in here — a lot to learn, and a lot that's hard to understand. It's definitely a good idea to go back over all this __thoroughly__, otherwise it'll all turn into a big tangled mess in your brain.

Revision Summary for Module P6

Electricity and magnetism. What fun. This is definitely Physics at its most grisly. The big problem with physics in general is that usually there's nothing to "see". You're told that there's a current flowing or a magnetic field lurking, but there's nothing you can actually see with your eyes. That's what makes it so difficult. To get to grips with physics you have to get used to learning about things you can't see. Do these questions to see how you're getting on.

1) Give a brief definition of: a) current, b) voltage, c) resistance. Write down the units for each one.
2) Sketch the standard test circuit. (In electronics, not Formula 1!)
3) Sketch the circuit symbols for resistor, variable resistor, bulb, cell, battery, switch and power supply.
4) Sketch a voltage-current graph for: a) a resistor, b) a filament lamp.
5) Write down the formula that links current, resistance and potential difference.
6) * Find the current when a resistance of 96 Ω is connected to a battery of 12 V.
7) Explain how potential dividers work.
8) State the formula for potential dividers. Do your own worked example, including a sketch.
9) Write down two facts about: a) variable resistors, b) LDRs, c) thermistors.
10) Give a definition of a magnetic field.
11) Sketch magnetic fields for: a) a current-carrying wire, b) a rectangular coil, c) a solenoid.
12) What is an electromagnet made of? Explain how you decide on the polarity of the ends.
13) Explain what is meant by "magnetically soft".
14) Make a sketch of the force on a current-carrying wire between two magnets.
    What is the name of this effect?
15) Explain how Fleming's Left-Hand Rule works.
16) Sketch a motor and list the four ways to speed it up.
17) What is electromagnetic induction? List four factors which affect the size of the induced voltage.
18) Sketch a generator, labelling all the parts. Describe how it works and what all the bits do.
19) What is a dynamo?
20) Give an example of how a dynamo can be used.
21) Sketch the three types of transformer, and explain how they work.
22)*In a transformer, the primary voltage is 6 V, the primary current is 10 A and the secondary voltage is
    3 V. What is the secondary current in the transformer?
23)*A transformer has an input voltage of 20 V and an output voltage of 16 V.
    If there are 64 turns on the secondary coil, how many turns are there on the primary coil?
24) Make a sketch of how transformers are used in the National Grid. Explain why power is transmitted at
    such a high voltage.
25) Write down three facts about isolating transformers.
26) Explain briefly how a diode works. What semiconducting material are diodes often made of?
27) Explain the two ways in which an AC current can be rectified.
    Include circuit diagrams and voltage/time graphs in your explanation.
28) What is a capacitor? How can it be used to smooth rectified voltage?
29) Draw truth tables for NOT, AND, OR, NAND and NOR gates.
30) Explain what is meant by a latch.
    Make a sketch of how two NOR gates can be combined to make a latch.
31) Explain how an LED can be used to show the output of a logic gate.
32) Make a sketch of a relay.
33) Go and read up on quantum theory... no wait, I mean... go and put the kettle on.

Answering Experiment Questions

Science exams nowadays are about more than just spewing out <u>facts</u>. You need to <u>apply</u> what you know to any context they might throw at you, and use all the information you're given in the question.

Questions on Experiments are Really Common

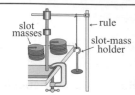

slot masses, rule, slot-mass holder

Jamie did an experiment to see how wires of three different materials changed length depending on the weight hanging on them. He took wires of the three materials, each with a length of 10 cm and a diameter of 0.5 mm, and hung a slot-mass holder from each one. He then gradually added slot masses until the wires broke. After adding each mass, he measured the new length. His results are shown in the graph below.

1. (a) Draw a line of best fit for Wire C.

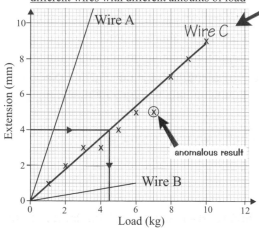

Scattergram to show the extension of different wires with different amounts of load

anomalous result

A line of best fit is drawn so that it's easy to see the <u>relationship</u> between the variables. You can then use it to <u>estimate</u> other values.

When drawing a line of best fit, try to draw the line through or as near to as many points as possible, ignoring <u>anomalous</u> results. In this case, it's also got to go through the <u>origin</u> (0, 0) as you know there'd be no extension without any load.

(b) Estimate the load Jamie would have needed if he wanted Wire C to extend by 4 mm.

Estimate of load = ...4.5 kg (see graph).........

(c) What can you say about the relationship between load and extension for Wire C?

Each additional mass caused the wire

to extend further.

In lab-based experiments like this one, you can say that one variable <u>caused</u> the other one to change. The extra load <u>caused</u> the wire to extend further. You can say this because everything else <u>stayed the same</u> — nothing else could have been causing the change.

Be careful with the word 'cause' though... to take an absurd example, if you do a survey on a beach, you may find that the number of people getting <u>sunburnt</u> seems to rise with the number of <u>ice creams</u> sold. But it'd be daft to say that buying an ice cream <u>causes</u> sunburn. It's due to a <u>third variable</u> — if the <u>sun is shining</u>, more people will want an ice cream, and coincidentally more people will get sunburnt.

(d) Which wire would you say was made of the stretchiest material?

Wire A

(e) Give one way that Jamie ensured this was a fair test.

The length of wire was the same (10 cm)

for each of the different wires.

To make it a <u>fair test</u>, you've got to keep <u>all</u> variables other than the type of material the same. Only then can you get a true comparison between the stretchiness of the three materials.

Another possible answer would be that the <u>thickness</u> of the three wires was the same.

(f) Why do you think the line for Wire B stops after 6 kg?

The wire must have snapped at 7 kg.

Use your <u>common sense</u> for this one. Also, it's always a good idea to read the question through again if you're stuck.

Index

Index

Answers